W9-CHR-418

Digging for Roots: Dalmo'ma 5

We wish to thank the following individuals for their generosity, encouragement and support, without which this collection would never have been birthed. We ask forgiveness of any individuals who have been omitted:

Linda Allen, Peter Allen, Greg Arnold, Patricia Bagley, Carol Jane Bangs, Steve Barbe, Ginger Barrett, Carol Bates, Ellen Beavers, Janet Bradstreet, Clifford Burke, Helen Byers, Hillary Carver, Kathy Dempsey, Rick and Larry Dennison, Alice Derry, Walter Dill, Lisa Enarson, Jack Estes, Cheryl Freeman, D.J. Hamilton, David and Judy Hartman, Steve and Janeen Hayden, Leslie Hayertz, Rachel Herr, Phyllis Hopeck, Sharon Howe, Candace and Raymond Hulbert, Melanie Humfleet, Tom Jay, Dierdrei Keegan, Ru Kirk, Jule Klotter, Carol Knebes, Claire Lasky, Maryna Lawson, Gary Lemons, Fran Lightbourne, Evelyn Livingston, Kelly Loftus, Dan Maguire, Heidi Mattern, Anna McEneny, Robin Miller, Larry Montgomery, Joyce Morden, Barbara Morgan, Dorothea Ammann Pares Morgan, Kay Myers, Rusty North, Gary and Mary Novak, Sharon O'Hara, Steve Oliver, Roberta Ossana, Barbara Pastore, Molly Pearson, Diane Pfaff, Frank Platt, David Prior, Kathy Prunty, Boots Randolph, Georgia Richard, Harlean Richardson, Judith Roche, David Romtvedt, Mary Lou Sanelli, Helen Shaw, Dick and Emmy Shipman, George Shearer, Leslie Oliver Siemer, Liz Svensson, Marian Taylor, Loretta Miles Tollefson, Liz Vickers, Cindy Wacker, Scott Walker, Sally Weinschrott, Pamela Whitney, Karen Wilks, Virginia Wolf, Cindy Wolpin, Merry Youle, Julie Zander, Marlene Zyvloski.

And last, but not least, The Paleolithic.

Copyright © 1985 Empty Bowl, P.O. Box 646, Port Townsend, WA 98368

Cover design by Helen Byers. Cover photo: Edward Curtis, "Woman Digging for Roots," courtesy Makah Cultural Center, Neah Bay, Washington.

ISBN 0-912887-13-3

Printing by McNaughton and Gunn

Quotes on back cover: *The Quotable Woman, An Encyclopedia of Useful Quotations,* edited by Elaine Partnow, Anchor Books 1978.

Table of Contents

Letter From the Editors

This anthology is a concrete expression born out of a mutual vision. We chose to focus on the narrow strip of land bordering the Strait of Juan de Fuca, summoning the hidden richness of women's lives. The "roots" represented here have their beginnings in pre-history, in historical accounts, in the fertile ground of the psyche, and in the mundane details of women's lives.

This anthology is our potlatch, our "give-away." It has been a renewal of our early feminist vision, gifting us with the opportunity to "pay-back" our psychic debts to the many women along the way who gave us the courage to take creative risks. Pass it on.

Our vision and our efforts formed the nucleus of an organism which claimed its own life, insisted on its own direction. Just as logs crashing into the rocky inter-tidal abrade settled life and established patterns *and at the same time* sweep clean wide areas which are then opened to new generations of plant and animal life, editing this anthology has had much the same affect on us, both personally and communally.

At times our vulnerability threatened us, but our work has been a commitment of the heart.

Susan Oliver
Christina V. Pacosz

August, 1984

i

Introduction

It is a commonplace among literary historians
that what literary works reveal of the times and
places that gave them their generation is often
as significant as the aesthetic pleasure they give
to a reader. As Merrill Lewis has pointed out,
the main importance of regional writing in the
last century may not have been the discovery of
local color or the regionalist's contributions to
literary realism but "the opportunities it gave
writers, especially women writers, to render the
condition of women in American society or to ex-
plore the woman's perception of reality."[1] It is
not so commonplace to encounter assessments of
contemporary writing which assume this same perspective. But that is precisely the perspective
I want to suggest to the reader of this anthology. The works here represent a small sam-
pling of the writing being done in our lifetimes
by women in a particular geographical region of
the United States—the Olympic Peninsula of Western Washington. The value of these pieces is
documentary; they reveal for us, in their variety
and complexity, the feminine consciousness in its
local frame, the feminine experience of a sense
of place and time. In this sense, these works are
already history, a slice of life placed in a literary time capsule, preserved for future generations.

Bernice Slote has said of Willa Cather, "[her]
works do not emphasize what is usual in the fantasies or myths of the West—cowboys, immigrant
trains, explorers and heroes, or the Plains Indians.
These did not have an immediate emotional impact
on her. Her central subject was historical, but
it was history in a low key."[2] This collection
might also be characterized as "history in a low
key." For the personal experiences, dreams, myths,
memories, and portraits collected here are not
meant to duplicate the records to be found in coun-
ty courthouses and military graveyards. It is a

different kind of history being made here, one
future generations might well value even more
highly. For it is the emotional impact of events
that defines our humanity, more than the events
themselves.

The remembrances, for example, of Marian
Taylor, the "Pack Train Grandmother," evoke experiences not only interesting in their own right,
but valuable in what they tell of the life of a
woman directly encountering the wilderness with
an aplomb any professional woman might envy. To
be a career woman on the Olympic Peninsula, she
tells us, doesn't necessarily mean wearing three
piece suits. Likewise, the memoirs of 92-year-old
Arie Anderson remind us of the hundreds of journals and diaries kept by pioneer women and now
housed in the special collections sections of
university libraries where students of the Western experience rub shoulders with students of
Women's Literature. What these recollections and
diaries tell us is what the history books leave
out: the everyday domestic life of previous generations and the inner thoughts of half of human-
kind.

If the diaries and journals of past centuries
can teach us about the feminine experience, it is
not surprising that contemporary women also turn
to the diary and journal as a means of plumbing
their own experiences, both external and internal,
physical and psychological. Thus it is that we
read here journals of travel, of self-examination
and self-confrontation, minutely detailed records
of women's lives. Sometimes it seems almost that
the process of recording the details is an attempt
to convince the writer herself of the reality of
her experiences, the consciousness turned on itself in Proustian self-examination and exploration.
Whether in Florida, Port Townsend, or Mexico, the
diarists and writers of personal records take as

their subject the feminine consciousness itself; they ask what it is to be a woman, to be a wife, a mother, a writer. Sometimes travel away from one's home lends the perspective needed to understand one's connection to place. In "The Passing of the Ohio" memories of India serve as a background and suggestive context for the looming significance of the presence of the Trident class submarine and the impact of the idea of the Trident on the consciousness of the writer. Whatever the Olympic Peninsula may be, this writer tells us, it is not a place of innocence. The Ohio will pass through our waters, entering our imaginations forever.

While it is perhaps more difficult to generalize about the poetry in this collection, it should be observed that it is in the poetry, more than in the prose, that the physical details of place take on a significance equal to or greater than the moods or observations occasioned by those places. In Ru Kirk's "Cafe Life," we perceive immediately the particular characteristics of small town gathering places (as compared to their big-city counterparts). This is a place where nature is always evident, rumbling outside the door, eating away at the foundations of human constructions, where

> Outside the cafes the short bay
> rises in winter's first winds and tides
> begins to take back this
> once sand bar, this now dog town.

As important as place is the experience of womanhood, the recogniton of the small events in life that loom large in human consciousness while rarely making their way into official chronicles of an age. Thus, in Alice Derry's "Peeling Apples," the feminine wisdom of three generations is

transferred over the routine motions so familiar
to those who do "women's work"; in this poem the
child is not unaware of the heritage she receives,
waiting until the women finish their stories and
go into the house, waiting to "practice, like
dressup/ try all the necklaces, drape on the jacket, the fringed shawl, the velvet cape lined
crimson." The poet here recognizes the richness
that is her legacy, even though it has been presented in humble context. That wealth hidden
within everyday experience shows up in many of
these poems.

In her book *The Female Imagination*, Patricia
Meyer Spacks suggests that there is a paradox in
the writing of many women who make for themselves
"no claim of special artistic ability or manifest
significance in the world." Taking as an example
an earlier Olympic Peninsula writer, Betty MacDonald,
Spacks suggests that in writing itself many women
may find an escape from their own life dilemmas.
In writing anything at all they are declaring their
own specialness, their own personal significance.[3]
But to write about their own lives is ultimately
to risk making those lives seem insignificant,
particularly when, like MacDonald, they resort to
self-deprecatory humor. It is, I believe, the
success of many of the writings in this collection
that the authors both convincingly assert their
right to speak for women, to speak for the feminine
experience, and yet retain a close attachment to
that experience, to the women who remain silent.

CAROL JANE BANGS

NOTES:
1. Merrill Lewis, "Preface," *Women, Women Writers,
and the West*, Troy, N.Y.: The Whitson Publishing
Co., 1979.
2. Bernice Slote, "Willa Cather and the Sense of
History," in *Women, Women Writers, and the West*.
3. Patricia Meyer Spacks, *The Female Imagination*,
New York: Avon Books, 1976, p. 282.

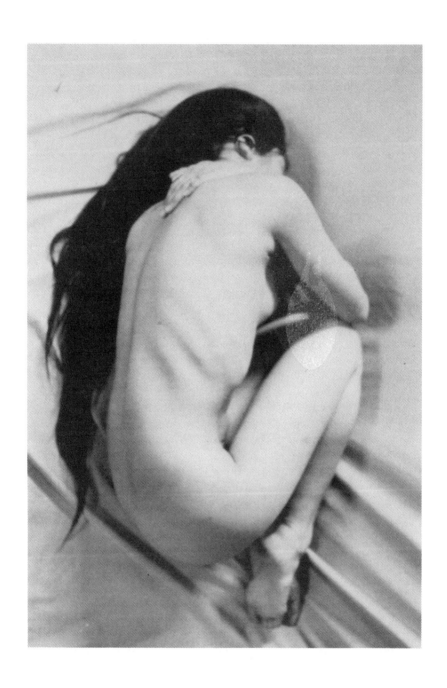

vi

The End of Summer

Leaning up against the wall, just inside the back door, was a piece of driftwood. It was shaped like a smokehouse ham and faded to a bone-white. Fitted over the wide, rounded end was a man's tube sock. The red stripes were stretched out thin and the empty toe flopped over like a topknot. Thinking back, Maggie remembered her casual acceptance of this odd combination. Her mom was a creative person and there was always some project lying around. This was just another original in the beginning stage.

Maggie closed the back door and turned into the kitchen, preoccupied with the conversation she was silently rehearsing. The words all crowded together in her mind, and seemed to press against her eyelids. She was nervous about this meeting. She and her husband had settled on a two-week separation in order to sort out their troubled marriage, now the time had come to discuss their future. Janos had been reluctant, but had agreed to stay in her mother's empty house. He felt that they should stay together regardless of the quality of the relationship; an attitude reinforced by his Catholic upbringing and his reverent attachment to his stoic parents who were still struggling with life in post-revolution Hungary. Maggie knew, deep inside, that they would not stay together.

The sound of a transistor radio buzzed around her as she walked through the kitchen. It was turned to the maximum volume, but because of the poor quality of the batteries, the music was reduced to fuzzy noise. Janos was washing his hands in the bathroom which angled off the kitchen, adjacent to a narrow hallway. The door was partially open and she waited for him to come out so she could use the facilities. They exchanged quick glances and a timid greeting as they passed each other. Maggie was grateful for the solitude of

the small room. The determination she had had
when she arrived began to waiver. She rethought
the words she was going to say and tried to
memorize the sequence she had worked out.

Janos seemed more withdrawn. He had always
been an inward man, one who considered emotional
expression frivolous, but now there was a change
that went beyond introversion—a depression. In
one of their discussions before the separation,
Maggie had asked him if he wouldn't be happier
back in his beloved country. Janos had stared
at her until tears overran his somber eyes. He
had come to the United States after the Russian
invasion of Hungary in late 1956.

Through the narrow streets of Budapest,
students, workers, and militia fought to free
their country of Russian domination. Most had
lived all of their lives under the eye of the
Red Star and in fear of the AVO, the Soviet
Secret Police. Janos left his factory job to
join the revolution. For seven ecstatic days the
people of Budapest celebrated freedom. When the
serpentine of Soviet tanks rumbled into the sleeping capital, Janos borrowed a bicycle and quietly
headed east toward the Austrian border.

Many of the freedom fighters eventually settled in Seattle. The young learned quickly and
enjoyed all that their new country had to offer.
Some of the older men and women found it harder
to adapt to the drastic change in language and
culture. Janos did not assimilate. In fact,
he created his prior lifestyle, enclosing his new
family in the traditions of his homeland. No
matter how much he may have longed to return to
Hungary, he could not. He had participated in
the revolt and the consequence was imprisonment
or execution. The Communist regime remained
harshly suppressive for many years after the
revolution.

Maggie glanced in the mirror as she dried
her hands and caught the look of apprehension which
had settled in her dark eyes. Had she looked like
that when she first arrived? She recalled the
expression she had seen on her husband's face as
they passed each other. His gaze had been direct,
but his eyes seemed as though they were focused
backward into his brain where he saw only himself.
There was a politeness to his mouth, but no smile.

She opened the bathroom door and the fuzzy
music again scratched the calm. As she stepped
through the doorway, heading back toward the kitchen, she caught a glimpse of the driftwood project hovering over her shoulder and knew Janos was
behind her in the narrow hallway. The sound was
a dry thud and Maggie hunched her shoulders against
the next blow. Nothing hurt, yet her legs could
not hold her up. She could feel the cold hard-
ness of the linoleum as it pressed against her
sticky back. There was a heavy weight on her
chest and her arms were rigid, pushing the hands
away from her throat. She closed her eyes and
mind. The single purpose of her body was to con-
centrate strength into her straining arms. There
was silence. Not a sound uttered from either
gaping mouth. She couldn't hear the heaving
breaths which blew warm on her face. She knew
the radio was still on, but the noise had gone
away.

Maggie's eyes opened. The pressure had
stopped. She saw the hands reaching beside her,
grabbing for the piece of driftwood. Vision
brought terror. Frantically, she arched her back,
rolled onto her side, and shoved Janos to the
floor. Maggie could see the back door and willed
it to come closer. Her legs worked only in slow
motion and the door was still too far away. She
thought about the automatic lock. Was the bolt
in place? She listened for footsteps as she

3

urgently twisted the doorknob. The door flew open and banged back on its hinges. Maggie jumped down over the steps and tumbled to the sidewalk. She listened, again, for footsteps, ear to cement, until she could pull herself up. As she stood, the brilliance of July spiked into her eyes making them sting. She found her way to the neighbor's porch and pushed hard on the doorbell. Again she pushed, harder this time. No one came.

Maggie could see herself in the faces of the people who drove past. Hair and dress matted with blood, no shoes, bare toes poking through ragged nylons. One hand, red and swollen, reaching out toward the road as if it were waving goodbye. A reddish lump of a person propped up on a porch.

When the police arrived, she was still sitting there. They asked her questions and she answered. They didn't seem to hear her when she asked them to check the house. Both officers waited with her for the ambulance. She could hear the siren, so faint and far away. She was startled when she looked up to find it parked by the curb, the white-clad attendants already opening the doors. She wanted to walk. She didn't want to get on the stretcher. She didn't want to lie down in the back. The driver let her sit up. Before the doors were closed, she again asked the policemen to check her mother's house.

At the hospital, one of the nurses removed Maggie's clothing. First the soaked dress, and then a cumbersome layer of pettipants, panty girdle, pantyhose, and finally, underpants. That part seemed comical to her and she thought she smiled. No one appeared to notice. She was wheeled down a pale yellow tunnel with dim cake-shaped lights moving overhead. She tried to count them but they made her dizzy. She lowered her gaze, not wanting to close her eyes.

Maggie felt detached, an impartial observer, as the huge x-ray machine rotated around her head. The technician impatiently attempted to position her, and she tried harder to pay attention to what he said. When all the films had been taken, she was left alone in the semi-darkness. Over the hum of the processing equipment, she heard muffled conversation punctuated by the occasional crackle of x-ray film. Two men in suits leaned into the room from the hall, apparently anxious to come in, but waiting for permission. A nurse brought them over and Maggie listened as they talked in low church-voices. One of them read to her from several sheets of paper and then asked her to sign the last page. She said no. The men exchanged a quick glance, patted her shoulder, and left.

She was taken out of the cool, dark room and back into the yellow tunnel. Maggie kept her eyes averted from the ceiling lights and squeezed them shut as the gurney turned into a room blazing with fluorescence. She was scooted sideways onto a narrow table. Tufts of hair floated to the floor as clippers whispered near her ear. She asked if there would be bald spots, the doctor assured her he would leave some hair to cover the shaved part. She was not convinced. The whirring stopped and the clippers were replaced by a long, gleaming needle. It stung into her scalp like an attacking wasp.

Her head was heavy and it wanted to roll down and rest on her collarbone. She let it rest and wondered if the bandages were lopsided. She was back in a wheelchair in yet another hall. Maggie's sister, Laura, and brother-in-law, Neal, were talking to the doctor. She could hear their voices and once in a while, words would float out of the office toward her...the medication..she'll sleep... tell her....

Laura stood awkwardly beside the wheelchair, gingerly stroking her sister's swollen hand. Neal tried to keep his voice steady as he told Maggie that Janos had hanged himself in the basement after she ran from the house. He told her that her four small children were safe, and he told her that she would not be going home for a while.

Somehow the summer ended. Fall came early and surrounded the city in shades of grey and gold. The cold, short days sent the neighbors retreating into the warmth of the houses. The callous and the curious would soon find other interests. Maggie and her young family could begin to put the horror behind them.

Maggie sat, legs curled up under her robe, on the couch and watched her two oldest children, fresh from their evening baths, stretched out on the carpet to read. Brother and sister, pajamaed shoulders touching, shiny heads close together sharing the privacy of a brightly colored book. Kati was five and would start school soon. Her long hair, fine as cornsilk, cascaded down her back, tucked behind small, pink ears. Gabi was four. His tan corkscrew curls pressed damp against his temples and tickled at the back of his neck. He and Kati were like twins—closest to each other. Three-year-old Anna cuddled next to Maggie on the couch, her sweet-smelling blond hair poked out in a crown of cowlicks. She pushed a book into her mother's lap and picked wisps of fuzz from her favorite blanket while she waited to be read to. Little Istvan padded over to the two lying on the floor, his molasses-colored hair, still wet, framed his chubby face. He stooped to point in the opened book, his heavily diapered bottom bobbing between sturdy baby legs.

As she watched her children, Maggie's eyes brimmed with wonder and devotion. She knew it was time to proceed into the future. Her strength

would be their security. Her actions would be
their indicators. Tomorrow night, she would not
bring her blanket and pillow to the couch. Tomorrow night, she would sleep in the master bedroom. It was a beginning.

FRANCES McEVERS

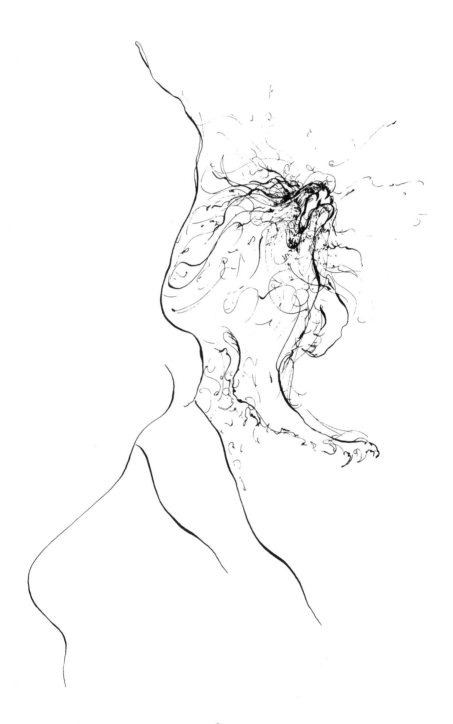

Sleeping Together

As if sleeping were together:
in each other's arms, our limbs numb,
and we stretch apart into dreams:
through a mirror you watch a hand
reach in a window and take the purse.
You stand in the kitchen with a butcher knife,
but you're helpless. I hear only your moaning
and wake you, press my sleep-dried lips to yours
once more, mouthing which is to teach us each other.

When the beat quickens, I'm pushed
inside the circle alone. They stomp and grin,
firelight on the sweating faces, you
one set of clapping hands holding me to the dance.

To the death, *then* to finally quit the mouth
which contemplates its kissing,
the stroking hand saying to itself, now
I am stroking him, and become *one*,
the ground gently assuming a body.

Instead, morning comes grey
at the curtain, and our faces
show lips, eyes, the shadows between.
I am on top so you can watch me,
and you keep saying, you're so happy,
you're so happy.

ALICE DERRY

My Mother Had No Sons

```
Asleep,
vulnerable in the half-light,
I touch my fingers
down the curve of his cheek
to caress the boy-sized
sucked thumb
fist
curled delicately outside his lips--
like the shells of the little garden snails
patiently tamed to slide wristward.
I don't want to love him
more,
just differently...
He's my son.
I guess I know my
daughters are equal to the pain
of the world,
and that men die
from it,
not outside, but inside,
becoming shell-bearers,
hardened and insulated;
childhood soft parts inward
snail-like.
```

PENELOPE GONZALES

Clytemnestra Resolved

Any affection I felt for my husband died with my poor daughter ten years ago. These long years have been entwined with rumors. Always present has been the rumor that my illustrious husband, the King, Agamemnon, was returning from Troy. But this time I believe the stories are true; I have received several messengers who can, who should be believed. He is finally returning. Oh, how I have prayed that he be killed in his bloody war, as now I pray that his ship be pulverized by the sea he bought with Iphigenia's life. I used to panic at the idea of his return, but the panic has dulled over the years. I know my choices and my mind is at rest.

Now that it is almost over, my memory revives gentler times that I've not thought of in years. The first time I saw Agamemnon I was so overwhelmed, so young, so naive. Not even fourteen, younger and more ingenuous than even Electra, I was easily impressed. He was so tall, seemed so noble. When my mother, Leda, told me a marriage was being arranged I was ecstatic. I did not know my worth then as the daughter of Leda, as the half-sister of Castor and Helen. Instead I daydreamed that he had heard of my talent, my virtue, my beauty and had fallen in love with me. How silly I was. I've tried to instill in Electra a sense of her importance, of her position in the House of Atreus. I've not insulated her from politics. It may serve her yet, though it may well be at my expense. She hates me, despises me. She is too proud of her father. Her sister's murder is only a story that people don't often tell in the palace. All she seems to know is that she is the daughter of the great King Agamemnon, victor at Troy. She is loyal to his memory and his name; and I, her mother, his wife, am not. I am afraid I have lost both my daughters and Electra will not have the opportunity to know her father for the barbarian

11

he is. If there was only a way to save myself
and not make a martyr of Agamemnon. Of course,
I could forsake my position, my lover Aegisthus
and become a priestess in a protected temple.
But I am genuinely fond of Aegisthus; I love him.
Perhaps more I love my position. I am Queen and
I will remain Queen. I have earned at least that
much from my marriage.

I sent Orestes away to a safe place years
ago. I miss him. But as Agamemnon's only son
I was afraid for him. I did not know if I could
protect him from his father's enemies, and I did
not know if I could trust Aegisthus. I did not
love him then, and I doubted his motives. Actually, I still do. Aegisthus is an ambitious man—
only an ambitious man, or a very passionate one,
becomes the lover of the Queen, a traitor. I
know his faults and weaknesses, but I chose him
with my eyes open. I was no lovesick, hero-
worshipping girl as I was when the king married
me. I do not blame Agamemnon for disappointing
my childhood fantasies. That was bound to happen. The bitterness might have passed with time
and maturity, even though my husband was selfish
and ruthless. I was beginning to understand him
and politics and my role as Queen rather than as
wife. Then my half-sister, Helen, was carried off
to Troy; and my brother-in-law, Menelaus, came
crying to Agamemnon, flaunting the family's
damaged honor. I was against Agamemnon going to
fight Troy. I was afraid I would not be able to
manage the kingdom in his absence; I was worried
about the future of our son, Orestes, should
Agamemnon be killed; and I was worried that Agamemnon would be killed and I would lose him. Even
then I clung to the shreds of the image I held
of him, his public image, the image I have unfortunately maintained in Electra's heart.

When servants brought me whispers of sacrifice

at Aulis, I did not believe them. Not at first,
but I did seek an audience with Agamemnon. He
was very busy, with maps and charts all over the
table, with advisors he was hesitant to dismiss.
He was irritated at my interruption, but I insisted. I told him I had heard strange things.
He laughed. He put his arm around me when I still
looked concerned. He said that the soldiers were
superstitious and restless. They felt Artemis
was turning the sea against them because several
soldiers had killed a deer in her forest. But
he had been told that the weather was to change
and so they would calm down. I asked if it could
possibly be true that they wished to sacrifice
our innocent daughter. He grunted a yes. I was
indignant and decried such stupidity and blood
lust. Surely the soldiers who had hunted the
deer were more likely a sacrifice to the virgin
goddess than a sweet, young girl. It was not
till later that I remembered his silence. He was
not often so indulgent. I wanted to be reassured,
and so it was simple for him to send me away calm.
I was such a fool.

The weather did not change. The mood of the
troops grew fouler. I was not admitted to see
the King; the King was too busy planning the campaign. Iphigenia was ignorant. I sheltered her
as I had been sheltered. I sought permission
to return home with her. All my requests were
denied. I was told that our leaving would damage
morale. I plotted to run away with my daughter,
but escaping from an armed camp, even if it is
your own, is not easy. I was frantic, even though
I could not yet believe that Agamemnon would allow anything to happen to our daughter. Then
I was isolated from Iphigenia. I was put under
heavy guard. Iphigenia was told that she could
not see me because I was ill, and that was easy
for her to believe. I had been so worried and

sleepless, I did not look well. In that desperate
isolation, all illusions withered. It was my
fault I had been reduced to such powerlessness.
I railed against my ineptitude. By trusting my
husband I had not adequately protected my children. I would never make such mistakes again.

Agamemnon gave the order and watched as the
priests stabbed my daughter. They sacrificed her
before an audience of bloodthirsty rabble who
could not wait to arrive at Troy to begin their
slaughter. He deceived her and then he watched
coldly. He asked her to accompany him to address
the troops, because I was too ill. Her maid told
me how excited she was as she dressed, how proud.
She adored him. I heard her scream. It ripped
through me with a violence I thought I was too
exhausted to feel. Then I heard the roar of the
crowd, and I vomited my grief and horror for
hours, but I could not rid myself of it.

By the time the sea calmed and the fleet was
ready to depart I was composed to play my part
as Queen, and in public. My husband was despica-
ble and repugnant, but I had two other children and
I would protect myself and them to the best of
my ability. That meant that Agamemnon must be
convinced of my loyalty in his absence. I mourned
my daughter; I could not dissemble that much, but
I mouthed pious words of a king's duty to his people and of appeasing the gods. I watched the ships
sail and cursed them under my breath. I returned
immediately home and began to rule, strong. It
surprised more than one person. I reviewed all
that I had witnessed since childhood, analyzed
it and began to practice it. I have become a
skilled politician. Certainly, it has been to
my advantage to maintain Agamemnon's image to the
people, and many long for his return. But it is
no secret that I have taken a lover. My power
is strong enough that I can handle that indiscre-

tion. The people are restless because Agamemnon
is soon to return, but I am reasonably confident
that those who do not love me or fear me, fear
the King enough so that he will arrive home in
ignorance. I cannot live with him again. If he
resumes rule over the country, my adultery, my
treason, will be made known, and I and Aegisthus
will be killed.

Aegisthus loves me. I don't know if he did
at first, or that he would if I were not Queen
of Mycenae. Occasionally we speak of running
away together, far away where we would be unknown
and could enjoy a quiet life. But we both know
it is just talk. Living with power is a part of
us and of our love. Nor would I desert my children. I have not, of course, had any children
by Aegisthus. Although our plans succeed, we
rid ourselves of Agamemnon, and we marry, I will
still have no more children. I will not jeopard-
ize Oreste's birthright by chancing more sons.
To be honest, I am not sure that I will marry
Aegisthus, poor man. Even once Agamemnon is gone
I must always remember to be careful. I, too,
have become ruthless.

My palace guard is made up of the young sons
left behind by their soldier fathers. They are
mature men now, well-trained and completely loyal
to me. I have reports that Agamemnon's fleet
has suffered many storms and lost many ships.
The few survivors will return from Troy weakened
and exhausted. I have planned a gay homecoming.
The people will turn out to see them and will
cheer them. Few will have returning relatives;
most will be drawn out by curiosity if nothing
else. I will greet them on the palace steps.
My welcoming speech is all prepared. My voice
will tremble with emotion, and that I will not
have to feign. My conscience is at ease, but
I am scared. I have dealt with many problems

these years ruling Mycenae, but admittedly, I've
had no opponent to equal Agamemnon. He was my
teacher in treachery, but now I must best him,
or I will die. I have information that he has
claimed the Princess Cassandra, the Trojan witch,
as his war prize. They and the battered remains
of his army will be ushered into the great hall
with all ceremony. I will have to risk sparing
several guards; tomorrow I will have them escort
Electra to another town until it is over. I
think that is best. I have assured her that according to my reports her father will not be here
for at least another month. I don't know what
she is thinking; she seldom speaks to me. As
soon as she is gone, I will give the kitchens the
order to begin preparing the feast. Agamemnon
and his company will eat and drink and tell stories
until they are drunk with the glory of their
long-dreamed-of homecoming. They are all the
murderers of Iphigenia and I will not hesitate.
My guards will be stationed throughout the hall
and at all the entrances. I will be closest to
Agamemnon. I will pull a dagger and I will kill
him. At that moment my guards will take over the
rest. When it is all quiet, as quiet as it is
here in my chamber tonight, it will be done, and
Iphigenia will be avenged, and I will be free.
In the following years Electra will come to understand and forgive, so I will regain at least one
daughter, my baby. And I will be able to send
for Orestes.

I have just received another messenger.
Agamemnon will reach the city in less than three
days time. After the runner has rested, I will
send him to Agamemnon with the news that I and
all Mycenae await his triumphant homecoming. It
has begun.

LESLIE HAYERTZ

16

Poem for the Poet

When I write
sometimes
I cry.

When I read
to an audience
I never
cry

though sometimes
as I am reading
I remember
the secrets.
This is where I choke.
This is where the tears flood

and then I see the poet Desiree
at the Open Reading Celebration
of the Mendocino Spring.
She was one line into her poem
before the packed house--
sister, sister, sister,
when her voice cracked
and the unpermissable
heaved in her throat
and she started
to cry.

The audience
died.

Desiree stopped. Regained herself.
She was wearing, she explained,
   her grandmother's dress.
She was saying her poem by heart.
She started again, *sister, sister*
Sister.
Again. The sob tore from her throat.
Again she stopped. Sister. Sister.
And then

the poet Desiree
was crying and crying and crying
and she couldn't stop.

The host came forward to help her off the stage.
I was the host. I said
Dorothy don't cry.
She cried Dorothy
is not my name! She cried
you must let me
say my poem.

She was wearing her grandma's red dress.
The front of it was getting wet.
Her tears were hard to take, it wasn't sad, it was
embarrassing
to see Desiree sobbing and sobbing like that.

So now beyond the wails of her long poem
we listened to the sea
tearing at the bluff, the cypress moaning on the roof.
The moon that night was full in Libra,
the Spring Equinox, the end of winter
in Mendocino
my town of Love, my town
of Grief, my town
of poets. And Desiree
crying and crying and crying.

Her lover, a famous poet, rose then from the audience,
came forward to help.
(Was the poem about him? we all wondered.)
But she pulled herself free of him, sobbing no!
No! No! Let me cry
my poem.

Her name at the time
was Eleanor.
It was after this poetry reading,
after this miraculous night

19

when the sun crossed the equator
that she changed her name
to Desiree.

The poem was about Paris.
The poem was about a child she gave away.
The poem was to her best friend
    she gave the child to.
Sister, Sister. She was growing
beautiful
crying the poem there in the Mendocino night,
  all that light
on her water, the Easter lilies and roses
swaying behind her
as she was sobbing
a tear for every word she knew by heart
ten tears for each poet in the house
one hundred tears for every orphaned child
a hundred tears for every lost love
a thousand tears for every crack
    in her broken heart
ten thousand tears for her vacant womb
a hundred thousand tears for the sea outside
    unloved and the land
and the cypress moaning a million tears
    for her brother,
the father. Father.

The poem went on forever.
She was in an airport trying to get somewhere.
She was crying sister! sister! sister!
Ten million tears for every sister she was crying
one billion *la-lou, la-lou, la-lou*

until we were swimming
in her water the light shone through.
There was danger we would drown
but not once
did Desiree ever say to us
I'm sorry.

She just sobbed and sobbed her heartbroken poem
into that rainy street in Paris,
a black woman in a red dress.

The lilies were bending so hard
in the equinox wind
the father of the child, an Osage Sioux
was rising from the audience
crying
I love you, I love you Desiree, I'm
sorry.

But Desiree is standing there
on the first day of Spring
shaking herself free.
(Though it is true they were married the next day.)
The tears are pouring
down her face.
Her dress is getting ruined, her nipples
are erect.
And the audience is drowning
and she is crying she's not sorry until we are all crying
and she is saying her poem by heart

sister   sister   sister
She is crying
la-lou   la-lou. My beautiful
la-louuuuu

· · · · ·

SHARON DOUBIAGO

Daughter Song

this is the field
I
dig with my hands
out here
by the red
red river.

Mother, you are my womb, my
own mouth
my
heart
bound together
we are each
what we owe
the
other.

Need
is my sharecroppers cabin
I am
always
one day too late.
what seed I sow
burrows inward
the bastard crop
bloody roots
to the air.

if
I could bring you my quota
would you kneel
on my vulgar front porch,
raise your fine dress?
can you
See us there together
my primitive face
a
wound
upon your benevolent breast?

I
drink deeply
and we are sharing that sweetest mixture
love and hate

confusion
the dark wine
of our survival.

LESLIE OLIVER SIEMER

They Call You Fetus

They call you fetus:
technical term for ligament, bone,
no ribbon-tie of life or love
between us.

They call you dead:
"fetal demise" packing away
long months of brooding, caring
into the attic.

You are these things.
Science will not brook denial
of its steel-blue facts,
sharp as ice,
unknowing.

You are all these,
and more:
still my child,
my little one.

LORETTA MILES TOLLEFSON

Upon a Miscarriage

They say I bear it well.
Death's done:
what's there to do but,
moving mutely to its beat,
continue on with life
and all the living, needing
round me?

They say I'll soon forget.
Heart knows:
the fruit,
however damaged by the frost,
is still the tree's.
She marks its drop.

LORETTA MILES TOLLEFSON

Riverside Drive

Her husband had brought home a game with little black doors and when you opened them a card would appear. You could play by yourself for hours. Charles Goren's Auto Bridge, it was called. It would be good with him gone so much, he'd told her.

"Playing with myself?"

"Learning," he'd said. "You can play with the wives from the ship then."

The only thing she despised more than card playing was not talking to an adult for days on end. So she learned the game that got her in a room full of women who matched paper napkins to bridge cards. They kept score on pads that also matched because there was a sense of order in having things around that matched with the husbands gone. She'd gone to have a drink or two without fear of becoming an alcoholic like the Exec's wife on that last ship her husband was on.

The women in the room with her were all wives of business men. Executives from big companies, like Bernice's husband, whose house it was, whose table she was at, wiping her mouth on a paper napkin that didn't match. Bernice's husband had averted his eyes on being introduced. She was used to that, men not making eye contact, silent about their guilt because they made too much money and because they'd give it all up for a chance to be absent themselves. Men whose companies sent them out of town for a day or two a month, who knew the taste of freedom and were envious. Of her husband, not of her.

It had nothing to do with her. Sure, there'd always be one when he'd found out her husband was gone who'd want to move in on her, but they were fewer than she'd expected. Because there was some kind of understanding men acknowledged that had to do with the wives of other men who were

27

gone that would not hold up with these same men
when the husbands came back. Some unstated
thing that they did not know about themselves.
With women it was different.

She was an outsider. The one who'd come into the neighborhood and would leave again. It
wasn't worth the effort to invest too much time
in being friendly with her. But she made an
even eight, enough for two tables of bridge and
that was why she'd been invited.

She was a beginner she'd said right off.
And they'd laughed, thinking she was being modest,
when she'd first come in and sat down. "I haven't
really played that much," she'd said next, after
her first big blunder. And they'd laughed again,
"It doesn't matter," they'd said, these women
who after a short time had made this much obvious:
there wasn't a one among them who wouldn't have
been as successful as their husbands and each of
them knew it. That was why they were there, giving the cards hell. An outlet. It was cutthroat
bridge they played. Bernice had been kind to
invite her.

She'd met Bernice while walking the baby.
Bernice had been working in her garden and she'd
stopped to admire it. Uncanny how she'd picked
up on things people took pride in. Bernice, a
reticent person, opened up with her, showing
her around the garden, acting friendly. Until
she'd mentioned to Bernice her husband was gone.
That made her suspect. A woman living alone
with four children, three under school age. She
couldn't possibly keep up her yard or house and
that would bring down the neighborhood. And
those children would hang around because their
father was gone, or worse, a pipe would break,
which sometimes did, and a husband would be
called, which she'd sometimes do.

That was why it had surprised her when a

28

few days later Bernice had called not asking but
telling her she played bridge. "All Navy wives
play bridge," Bernice had said, sounding exactly
like her husband when he'd presented her with the
game. A dumb game she'd wished she'd never got
started on. Having given it up she was forced to
take it up again when the loneliness got too much
for her. Sure, she'd said, she'd love to play.

The street where Bernice lived, two streets
over, had larger, more expensive homes. What the
real estate lady had called executive homes.
There were no executives on her street. Riverside
Drive, which sounded scenic in the ad, turned out
to have a snake-infested stream of murky water
running beside the house they'd rented. It was
the first house the real estate lady had shown
them and they took it because her husband's orders
had read "report immediately." San Salvador, the
island where Columbus had landed, not the city
as she first had thought, was where he was to be
stationed the next year. Without dependents, of
course. That was the reason for them coming to
Orlando. It was an hour's drive from where the
plane would bring him on weekends. One weekend
for every six weeks spent on the island.

Riverside Drive was inhabited by truckers.
Men with their own rigs whose wives were alone
for much of the time but the difference was they
had their families living in the neighborhood.
Most of the people on the street were related in
some way, so they all looked out for one another.
She would see them going in each other's houses,
the men with their left arms, the one that hung
out of the truck window, browner than the other.
Thin men, like their women and children, with flat
moon faces. They would wave to her but none of
them ever crossed the street to her. She'd been
left alone enough to be familiar with signs like
that, to know what they meant. So she stayed to

herself, learning their names off the mailboxes
so as to have something to write in the blank on
the cards the school passed out, where it asked
who to notify in case of an accident, because she
didn't know what else to write.

It wasn't until she was in the house about a
month or so before she'd come face to face with
any of them, or rather one of them, she'd seen
only the feet of the other man. She had come home
from shopping with all four kids in the car, the
boys in the back and the baby up front, and as
she pulled into the driveway the car made a terrible noise. She parked in the carport, too
tired to worry, and after unloading the children
and the packages she went into the house. In
the kitchen, putting away the groceries she heard
what sounded like someone hammering. The jalousies
on the side door were open and she went over and
looked out. She could see a man's feet sticking
out from under her car. The man they belonged
to was talking to another man out of her view,
asking him something. She saw a hand reach down
a pair of pliers.

She went out and stood on the top step, but
the one, the man who had handed down the pliers,
just barely turned his head and then he got down
to help the man under the car. She thought about
going in and bringing them coffee or something
but the more she thought about it the more she
realized it would be the wrong thing to do. She
thanked them but didn't know if they heard
her. She went back inside. After they left,
she was still standing there behind the jalousies,
silently crying.

Playing bridge at Bernice's she brought up
the incident with the car. She mentioned the
family, the one whose name she'd copied off the
mailbox, but neither Bernice nor the others said
much. They knew the family by name only, they said

and then they got on with their cards.

She played once a week, on Thursdays. The rest of the week she'd take her iced tea out on the screened back porch when the children were asleep and watch television. She'd go out in her nightgown with nothing over it, there being nothing behind the house but orange trees. Before her move she'd never seen an orange tree. A tree where green fruit grew alongside of the ripe, on the same branch as its blossoms, not in sequence but simultaneously. Without regard to order. Without the lapse of time it ordinarily took for a tree to go from flower to green and finally ripe fruit. She would stand out back on the property line mornings when she'd first get up, and it was as if she was in some other place. Some mythical land where all time was simultaneous, without present, past, or future as she knew it. Without the dull wait, the terribly long weeks between one plane landing and the next, where all time was one. That was how it was meant to be. Before things got imperfect. Like in the stories she'd read as a child, how idyllic the world was before man. And the trees were left behind as a reminder.

She could smell the blossoms and the acrid scent of the rind forming, the fruit ripening, all this at her back as she watched the late night news. She heard an owl in the distance and another noise and she got up and without turning off the television she went into the bedroom. The light was off and she could see out into the darkness.

"There's a Peeping Tom in the neighborhood," she said the following Thursday at Bernice's. Actually she was angry with them for not telling her about it. Because they knew. She'd watched their reactions, both tables. Saw each make a mental check on their own husbands and then look back at her as though from the other side of those little black doors she'd opened and closed

31

so often in the process of getting to where she
was now, at this bridge table, one hour's drive
from where the plane would land with her husband
one weekend for every six weeks spent on San Salvador, the island, not the capital. Then it happened. She didn't see it with her eyes but she
could feel it. Some closing up of the group,
like when a pack of wolves feels threatened.

They were eating the cake Bernice had
served. Bernice served cake, never liquor. This
was chocolate. One woman ate hers icing first,
separating it neatly from the cake. "They're
harmless," she said, "I read somewhere...."

"Well, I don't know that. He has that advantage on me. To even things up, I'm making
sure he is."

"What do you mean?" that same woman asked.

"I have a gun," she said, "my husband's,
and if he comes back I intend to use it."

"You can't shoot a man unless he breaks
into your house." That from Bernice.

"I'll shoot him first and drag him in,"
she said. Then both tables came down on her.
She didn't care. She might have cared a few
months back when she'd first come into the neighborhood but that was then. She'd almost died
since then. It was on one of those nights when
she sat out on the porch, before she'd discovered
the man behind the orange tree. In fact, she
probably would have ignored the sound he made
when his foot came down on the trench the boys
had build for their G.I. Joes. It was hot, the
night she was remembering. She had taken a sip
of her iced tea and a sliver of ice got caught
in her throat. She started to choke on it. While
she was coughing, trying to catch her breath,
she thought of what would happen if she didn't
come out of it, the things the baby could get
into before anyone ever found her. She could

feel herself losing consciousness, did for a moment, her mind a blank like the card the school had sent home. That was how she knew she was coming back out of it, she could see the card, "in case of accident." Not even that was on it. A blank. Then it was over. The ice had melted in her throat or maybe dislodged itself, but she could breathe again. That night she stayed up taping her husband's address and a phone number on the refrigerator and in the bathroom on the medicine cabinet. And later, in bed, trying to block out in her mind how long it would take him to arrive, it came to her. *She was the only parent her children had.*

She didn't tell that to the women. She didn't tell them the gun was a pellet gun, and that it was out of cartridges since the last time her husband was home when he'd used it for target practice on a cottonmouth. It was in a box on the shelf in her bedroom closet so even if she did know how to use the gun, by the time she got it down it would be too late. She didn't want to hurt anyone. What other way to enlist the help of these cake-eaters? Word would get out after tonight and she could sleep instead of watching out her window or listening from her bed. She'd been deliberately antagonizing to the women and hated them for it. She played every card in her hand right that night but left the cake untouched.

Things were strained after that but that didn't stop her from coming Thursdays. If they wanted her to quit they were going to have to tell her. Instead of them laughing politely when she made a mistake she was met with cold silence, but then they had to admit the mistakes were fewer. She became quite good at bridge in spite of herself, or maybe to spite them. They all showed up regularly to see if she'd come.

One week she called Bernice to say she couldn't play. She told her Donnie was sick, which was true; she didn't care if Bernice believed her. She kept Donnie home from school and that evening he ran a fever. Tired from taking care of him all day she went to bed early. She had just fallen asleep when he'd come in and woke her. His eyes were glassy and he was saying things like, they're coming to get us, Mom, we have to get out. She thought he was sleep walking until she felt his forehead. He was burning up and screaming by this time, "They're coming to get us!" She threw him into the shower with his pajamas on and stayed up most of the night trying to get the fever down. Then when she couldn't stay awake any longer she went back to her bed. The frogs had stopped croaking but there was another sound. When she heard it the second time, she thought of getting up but that was all, she was too tired to move.

It was the baby-sitter who told her about the man, that next morning.

"He was in your backyard, didn't you hear?"

"Hear?"

"Last night. They caught him and beat him up. Right back there in your yard."

The men who did the beating up were from Riverside Drive. The man across the street and two of his brothers. She wanted to thank them but it was the same thing as them fixing her car. That thing she picked up on in people, that had to do with what they took pride in. Like Bernice and her garden. What was different with the men was it lost a little something if they were thanked or too much was made of it.

If her suspicions were right about it being one of the husbands of the bridge players she would never know. She tended to think it was the one who ate her cake icing first, her husband.

Or Bernice's. She might have misread his look,
that averted eye. Or maybe none of them.
      She went out back by the property line
where the boys had built their trench for their
G.I. Joes. The trench was flattened now from
where she imagined a man's body was held while
being beaten. By that narrow line that separated
the yard on Riverside Drive from the orange grove
she stood, her eyes not on the trench but ahead,
on the trees overladen with blossoms and fruit
and whatever it was they used to remind her of.

                                    EVELYN LIVINGSTON

Peeling Apples

I sit under grandma's walnut tree.
She and mother are in chairs,
a bushel of gravensteins between them.
They talk and I listen, or we're all silent,
our mouths slackening and pursing
for the hands: knives snap an apple
in two, in four, dip to core each quarter,
strip the peeling, done. Three sets
of hands: mom's seamed with years of cutting,
grandma's lumpy too from arthritis, mine,
clean, inept, waiting for Sunday dinner
when dark brown applesauce will be handed round
in small gold and pink-rimmed saucers.

I hate peeling but crave the talk,
thirteen, still in braids, long-legged,
outraged into silence by my body's changes,
tolerated here for the apples' sake.
Through my thick glasses, I dream into the gossip
and try to keep up: women's work, its efficiency,
the least number of moves. They treat their friends
to the same: tight-lipped stories with morals.
I wait for one more to marry, give birth, take ill.
When they go in, I practice, like dressup,
try all the necklaces, drape on the jacket,
the fringed shawl, the velvet cape lined crimson.

ALICE DERRY

Las Vegas, 1951

My father wakes me gently,
leads me to the back yard,
checks his watch
in the faint neon glow.
I wiggle my bare toes
in damp grass, and yawn.

Then the black rumble:
cottonwoods rustle windlessly,
windows chatter like teeth,
the earth bucks and totters
beneath our feet, my hand
aches in Daddy's steady grip.

Look, he whispers, and points
northwest, where the cloud rises
with the sun, glows and billows,
and blooms on its thick stem,
cumulus amanita
in a pastel Nevada sky.

We stand becalmed, hand
in hand under the spreading cloud,
snapshots of ourselves
in a soundless world. I wonder
about my turtle, lost last week
in a patch of unmown clover.

Then a dog barks, a cricket
chirps staccato from the bushes,
a car purrs by, and I
leap into warm air,
dancing my bravado, pulling
against my father's silence.

We walk into the kitchen
where Mother stands by the stove
pouring cups of coffee,
stirring in cream and sugar,
and even before she turns
I know she will be weeping.

MAGGIE CRUMLEY

Crossroad Seven

When I was five I found
an obscene woman crouched
beside the road,
naked and unclean,

all tangled in
beauty and forever.

and as if she were a lost doll
I gathered her
all into my rocking arms,
and staggering
with love and fear and duty

left the road and found
a far path bushwhacked by
a billion stars.

GEORGIA RICHARD

That Good Night

Two carts of breakfast trays clatter down
the long corridor from the kitchen to the nurse's
station in an uneven roll of metal wheels and
jangle of glass and silverware. Half-asleep in
the dim, artificial light of the nursing home's
bottom level, Melissa urges herself to join the
other aides in the early morning ritual. Her
need to help, to heal, to make it better propels
her. Rubber-soled shoes squeal against brown
linoleum. Lights, the only alarm clocks, snap
on. Hospital beds hum upright, carying their
groggy occupants. The smells of strong, hot
coffee and grape jelly overcome the ubiquitous
odor of stale urine and disinfectant.

Melissa matches the pace of the more experienced aides as she rushes a half dozen trays into
rooms before stopping to feed a disabled patient.
After these summer weeks of work, she can feed a
stroke victim without spilling egg onto the hospital gown or dribbling orange juice down a chin
with an impatient tilt of the glass. All the
basic nursing skills that she learned spring
semester are natural to her now.

Within a half hour, breakfast ruins wheel
back to the kitchen. The seven nurse aides crowd
into the walk-in linen closet like worker ants.
Melissa waits for the counting and grabbing of
linens to dissipate. There will be enough, un-
like the nursing home that she knows of in which
one washcloth must service several patients.
She could never work in a place that treats its
patients like that. Nursing is a sacred calling
to her. It epitomizes service to others, a lesson that she internalized through countless
Sunday sermons.

Melissa lifts the heavy smoothness of
laundry-worn sheets from a shelf and picks up
clean, raveled towels. How lucky to get this
job at Oakmeadows! She's learned more about

nursing, about helping people, about individuals this summer than in all of her anxiety-filled hours of study and test taking. She exits the linen closet, closing the door behind her, and treks the long, beige-walled corridor,which glows with morning sun from the open doorways of the eastern rooms, to her first patient, to Sarah.

Girding herself for what she'll find, Melissa halts at the shadowy threshold of a double room. One half of the room mirrors the other: twin, oak formica, bedside cabinets; twin, rectangular tables to wheel before the patients' beds like portable desktops; twin, low, vinyl armchairs for the occasional guest; four, shadow-white walls and a cold, linoleum floor. Off-white, thermal blankets cover the two hospital beds. Only the second bed is occupied.

She sets the clean linens on the empty bed and crosses the room to raise the window blind. Indirect morning light drifts through the window to rest on a cloud of soft white hair that billows above an oval, porcelain face. Sarah's eyes open, a pale blue entrance to a sphinx. The blue stare stretches disinterestedly into space, not a flicker to acknowledge Melissa's presence.

Silent, Melissa gathers a towel and washcloth and retrieves a plastic washtub from Sarah's closet. She fills the tub with warm water in the adjoining bathroom. Does Sarah know that she's here? Melissa can't tell. Where is that low, resonant voice that had so impressed Melissa in early June with its intelligence? Melissa centers the tub on Sarah's oblong table.

"Sarah? Good morning." She searches for some sign of recognition, for some acknowledgement.

Melissa dips the cloth into the water and wrings it out. "It's Melissa, Sarah. Do you remember me?" She senses a hint of impatience in the sealed lips. The vacant stare does not waver. Has she done something to incite Sarah's anger?

Melissa runs the wet cloth uncertainly over Sarah's face, then wipes it dry. This Sarah awes her. The conscious strength of her will maintains that moribund silence, not a stroke-damaged brain. Melissa loosens the hospital gown and covers Sarah's smooth-skinned body with a sheet to prevent cold, to shield Sarah's dignity. Melissa soaps the cloth lightly as she washes and dries each limb and her chest. Not a muscle twinges in cooperative effort.

Upon finishing, Melissa heaves Sarah onto her side. Her arms and shoulders strain to move Sarah's leaden heaviness. Her shoes slip on the smooth floor momentarily until they brace for the weight. She disbelieves the onerous power of a body the size of her own average build. Irritated admonitions from other aides, angered by Sarah's lack of cooperation, lie on Melissa's tongue; but she will not repeat them. Something like love battles with the anger, soon to drown in frustration. Sarah has no right to do this, to reject Melissa's caring, to reject life.

Tar-like diarrhea, black from iron supplements, covers the plastic-lined disposable pad beneath Sarah. With lengths of toilet paper and, then, soap and water, Melissa cleans red, irritated buttocks as Sarah, uncaring, lies on her side. Melissa spreads lotions on the skin and centers a new pad on the bed, glad that the unsoiled sheet does not need to be changed. She eases Sarah onto her back. The fierce stiffness of Sarah's arms hampers an easy replacement of the hospital gown.

Melissa straightens the bedcovers and pulls them to Sarah's shoulders. Melissa gazes down at her; her dark eyes tear. "Why, Sarah, why?"

she whispers. "Why are you doing this to yourself? To me?" Sarah's eyes close to dismiss
her.

After lunch, Melissa leans against an insti-
tutional green wall between two, nodding patients
in wheel chairs. Before them, the lounge television drones a game show. Her feet throb with
six hours of baths, bed making, and travel down
long halls. Soon, the patients dotting the lounge
will ask to return to bed for naps.

Ms. Spencer, the director of nurses, beckons
to her from the doorway. "I understand you had
Sarah Harris today," she says when Melissa joins
her. "Did you notice anything unusual?"

Fogged images from dozens of patients and
dozens of mornings clear to a shadowed Sarah.
"Not really." How to explain that Sarah's
purposed lifelessness has become the norm?

Ms. Spencer nods. "I thought you would
have reported anything. On medication rounds,
the nurse found her dead."

"But she was..." Melissa bites off her ob-
jection and smothers her anger. Who is she angry
at? Sarah for dying? God for the pain? Yes.
She does not know how to accept death.

"I've contacted her doctor and her daughter. I need an aide to prepare the body. Since
she was your patient today," Ms. Spencer pauses.
"If you don't want to, one of the other aides
can—"

"No." Melissa denies the escape. "I've
read the procedure. I'll do it."

Sarah doesn't look dead yet, only very calm,
far calmer than Melissa has seen her in these
last weeks of suppressed tension. The skin feels
cold. Fearful that thought will flood her compo-
sure, she does not hesitate. Melissa cleans and
diapers the body; how strange that the last organ
to stop functioning is the intestines. She

follows the procedure automatically as if she has performed it every day for weeks.

Melissa opens the cabinet at the bedside to remove Sarah's belongings. In the table drawer, Melissa finds two pictures: a portrait of a young man in an antique frame, and a snapshot of Sarah with three grandchildren. The afternoon in which Sarah had shared those pictures flashes into Melissa's head. The man, Daniel, gave Sarah the picture two years before their marriage— his first and finest gift, she had said. The middle grandchild has Daniel's deep eyes and dimpled chin.

A Bible, a confirmation gift from her god-mother, lies beside them, the leather age-cracked, the gold lettering worn to faint outlines. The beginnings of a pink and rose-colored afghan fill the back half of the drawer. Sarah had asked her to put it there the day after Sarah's birthday, June 24. Melissa removes the yarn and remembers Sarah, erect patience as she waits for Melissa to help her out of the wheel chair and into bed for her nap.

"Seventy-five years is long enough." Sarah's matter-of-fact words resound in the room. "I can no longer walk. The body slowly shuts down. And this place, this place will very likely be my... my residence for the rest of my life." The words soften to a thought. "It is taking too long." Sarah stopped communicating after that.

Melissa stacks the pictures, Bible, and knitting on the empty bed. Is that why? She approaches Sarah's bedside, searchingly. Is that what made her take death?

But Sarah isn't there to answer. She isn't there. And it strikes Melissa what a terrible amount of living goes into death.

JULE KLOTTER

The Sounding Line

This red kerosene lantern, like a smoking
beacon, swinging wide between us, lighting
one side only of our conversation
spawns a thousand lanterns
mirroring our rhythm

in a thousand rivulets tethering sea
to shoreline with their braided luster
where the still bay stretches
towards a full moon buoyed
on its own reflection

and a fringe of sea whips lies like compass
needles left to point out tankers, listing,
bound for China on the thin horizon
while we follow midnight
and our frenzy deeper.

....

I will brave the shallows of this moonlit
harbor. I will wade out backwards, cast
at your instruction towards a chill
submersion, holding to the timbre
and the intonation

of your voice unfurled across the ebbing
water, sure and irresistible as any siren's.
Let the North Star falter. I will keep
my bearings, trusting only words
to reel me back in after.

....

Should the tide turn in now and, in shifting,
claim me, should cold, dark appendages compel
me under where the whorling firmament
blurs as I plummet, I will
stir a devil's dance

of sand around me when I settle,
sprawled upon the sheer blue silence.
Then my voice will rise up through
the muck and mire, cased in
spheres, in splinters

straining for the surface. Every syllable will
make its own way, drifting. Some will catch
at seaweed. Some will linger, latching
to the glint of candlefish, of sole,
or flounder. Others, rising higher,

snag upon the feathers of a tern emerging
from its blind dive, soaring. And the fluted
wake of my imagination will disperse,
like so much foam, those last few
bursting syllables remaining.

. . . .

Thus my voice will meet your own across
the fathoms and I'll climb that line between
us through the surface, grasp
the last firm knot, a gasp,
our breath commingling,

if you'll only call me to the shimmering
circle where the lantern light illuminates
one speckled starfish prying, prying,
prying yet another shell
eventually open.

MELANIE HUMFLEET

45

Pioneer Life

*These recollections of Arie Anderson's life
have been recorded, word for word, by Janie
Roberts. Arie felt these events should be
handed down to younger generations. In the
words of Arie Gotcher Anderson, as tears rolled
gently down her cheek, "I have lived in hard times
but I'd live them over again."*

Arie Anderson asked to include this
in the opening of the story.

My Dream Unveiled

When I was a very small girl, I liked to be
alone and walk as far as my fancy carried me.
I would leave the house and go past the highway (as my father called it) and into the alfalfa
field. There was an old log left from the log
cabin which had been the foundation of an older
log cabin. Wonder who lived in it and why?
I was just a dreamer. In the springtime I
went as far as my little legs would carry me.
I combed the field for springtime wild flowers
which were a joy to me. The flowers I used to
pick were called "Grass Widow." I would pick
as many as my small hands could hold and go
back to that old log and rest. Finally I would
take them home for my mother to put in water.
As the spring faded into summer, I still
continued to find solace in the old log where I
seemed to dream. It was such a mystery to me.
In the same spot there were two fruit trees. I
thought they were there just for me. One tree
produced large juicy dark blue plums. The other
was an apple tree. I was overwhelmed with the
plums. The apples were good also. I can't remember having taken any of the plums to the house.
But I will never forget seeing my mother coming

with a large bucket on her arm and watching her
fill the bucket with those plums.

The Promised Land

Father Jessie A. Gotcher was four years old
when Granddad, Jessie Newton-Gotcher, reached
the promised land—Williams, Oregon. As Granddad Jessie would say, "So many rivers and some
horses drown. They would unload the wagons,
throwing out the spinning wheels and irons. Lots
of horses died on the trail. They used up every
bit of their strength in their bodies." On the
covered wagon trails, many animals traveled with
the people. The reason was no grocery store to
stop at for the things they needed. If they
needed butter, the cow they brought, they stopped
and milked her, then sat in the back of the wagon churning butter with delight.

My father, Jessie A. Gotcher, was married
to my mother, Fannie Chastain. My father was
21 years old and my mother 17 years old. They
had five children: two girls, Arie and Mary
Gotcher-Stamateou, three boys, Newton Gotcher,
Glen Gotcher, and Walter Gotcher. Newton now
lives in East Grande, Arizona. Both Glen and
Walter are deceased.

Mary Arrives

I saw my father tie the horse at the first
gate and fly to the house. I sensed that he
was pleased. His face wore a grin from ear to
ear. Father said to me, "I have come to take
you home with me. You have a baby sister. Her
name is Mary. She is named for my grandmother
Mary Hushawl-Brown."

He had brought Aunt Lottie and Eunice with
us to see the new baby. We arrived at mother's

bedside and saw a little bundle wrapped in pink.
My mother opened the bundle, surprise! There was
a tiny little baby named Mary. Then my brothers
came for a look. Glen and Newton brought the
pink outing flannel. Mother had not been able
to sew. So she had hired a lady neighbor to
make them. Mary wore the night clothes until
she was two years old. At that time I was six
years old. Aunt Lottie wanted me to go home
with her. I was perplexed. Should I go with
them or remain home?

Farm Life

Neither Mother, sister Mary, nor myself
were allowed to work in Father's garden. That
work was for my father. It was his hobby.
Father ran a dairy business. After milking
there was a creamery to take our cream to process
it into butter. Many times I've seen my mother
work the water out of the butter. And you have
never seen such a large churn in your life. While
churning, mother often got thrown off her feet
and landed on the floor. Often my father did
the churning. The fresh-made buttermilk was something to drink. In those days, they had no
refrigeration. Instead, my father had built a
sawdust house for "anything that needed refrigeration." A sawdust house is made of walls that
are filled with sawdust. My father home-butchered
the hogs on the farm. I remember him dressing
them out and cutting up the hog slabs to be sold
as smoked pork.
My father had practically 100 acres in
alfalfa. That would have been horse heaven for
any horse.
My industrious mother was close at hand for
my father. There wasn't anything she could not
do if she wanted to. Mother was not particularly

49

fond of cooking. I was fond of cooking. And
mother let me take over the kitchen. At an
early age, I remember cutting out cookies and
biscuits when I had to stand on a box.

Harvest

In Grants Pass, Oregon, the threshers visited
the house. The hungry mouths were coming from
the fields to eat. I baked pies and cakes the
day they were to arrive. When it came to preparing the dinner, my father took a 5 gallon bucket and gathered corn on the cob plus beets primed
to be parched and then he dug the fresh potatoes.
The threshers seemed quite satisfied.

My mother was a perfect dressmaker. At an
early date she started to teach me her art. I
just couldn't do it as perfectly as she wanted.
It made me very unhappy.

When the time came for me to leave Grants
Pass to become a teacher, I was in my first year
in high school and I made a dotted dress. When
I returned home after school, I proudly displayed
the dress. My mother was so pleased. I felt
good inside knowing that I was able to please
her.

Courting

I had come home from school and was to return in a short time. I had not expected Rowland
to come to visit me. I heard the train stop;
we lived near. Before I could look to see who
had gotten off, I looked up and there he was.
He went back to Places, that evening. In a
short time I had returned to school.

On one evening Rowland had ridden a motor-
cycle in to meet me, to present me the engage-
ment ring. It was a lovely diamond and I accepted
it. I little dreamed that 7 years must pass before he could put the wedding ring on my finger.

ARIE ANDERSON as told to JANIE ROBERTS

A Makah Biography

*Following are several excerpts from the life
of Helma Swan Ward, a prominent Makah Indian
woman, who has been active in the traditional
and ceremonial life of Neah Bay, Washington,
for most of her life. Mrs. Ward's story has
been recorded by Professor Linda J. Goodman of
Colorado College, who is presently turning the
work into a book.*

In the 1920s when I was little, Neah Bay
was quite a bit different than it is now. There
weren't so many houses in the back. All the houses
were close to the front—near the water. We had
just a sandy street then—no blacktop road. Some
of the older people that I really didn't know too
well lived on the beach. They had little, little
houses down there which I can vaguely remember.
They were old-looking houses—no paint, no nothing—made out of wide boards.

We lived near the west end of the village
at a place they called Spanish Fort. The house
I grew up in was a two-story wood house built by
my dad. The land was my great-grandmother's.
She ended up giving it to my dad because she lived
with us until she died. She took care of him when
he was little, then when she got old, he took care
of her; he never let her want for anything. She
must have liked us kids because she took good
care of us, too.

Being brought up all Indian, my great-grandmother would never sleep on a bed, never sit on
a chair. As old as she was, she always sat cross-
legged on the floor of the house. Sometimes she'd
sit on the featherbed which was in the corner of
the living room where she always slept. She had
a real nice, thick featherbed, and I'd just flop
on it and sit and talk to her. She'd either sit
on that or on cattail mats on the floor. She was
real good about feeding me—fish or apples or

oranges. Then I'd sit and talk with her, and
sometimes she'd make me toys to play with if I
asked her. Most of the time though, she'd be
busy making baskets or cutting up fish or drying
fish. Often she'd go out to the big shed behind
our house, build a fire there, spread her cedar
bark mats out, and sit by the fire and make baskets. One by one, other old people would stop
by, join her by the fire, and sit there and make
baskets. I used to run in and out of there,
watch them, and visit with them. I really enjoyed those days.

My mother was also a very hard worker. She
worked just like a man, right along with my dad.
He started teaching her early, because ever since
I could remember she was a carpenter, a bricklayer,
she used to shingle houses, and eventually she
went into plumbing. He did all these same jobs,
working for the Bureau of Indian Affairs in Neah
Bay, and she worked right along with him. She
worked for many years and didn't get any money
for it.

Since my mom was working all the time with
my dad, I was needed at home to take care of the
kids. Ever since I could remember, I took care
of my younger brothers and sisters. I had to
have a baby tied on my back almost all the time
when I was working. My mother or grandmother
would tie one on me. They would make a triangle
out of a shawl, fold it so it was on the bias,
then cross it over my shoulders and under my arms
and tie a knot under the baby's bottom.

In the spring I had to get up early in the
morning to help my mom in the garden. She would
tie one baby on my back and I'd be holding the
hands of two others and I still had to weed the
garden with her. While she did the hoeing, I did
the weeding. I made the toddlers play on each
side of me, and if one took off, I'd have to go

and bring him back. The "baby-est" one I had to
carry on my back all the time. Mom would only
take the baby off my back when I got all wet in
the back. Then it was time to take the baby off
and change it.

I must have been about eight years old when
I was doing all of this, and one time I got so
mad I said, "Why do I *always* have to take care
of them!?" My mom wouldn't explain. My grandmother was the one. "Sit down," she said, "I'm
going to tell you why. Your mother is bigger
than you and she can work faster than you can.
If she had to depend on you to do all this work,
it would never get done." Seems it was always
left to my grandmother to tell me these things.
Maybe that's why I didn't get rebellious with my
mother, because my grandmother used to tell me.
She never told me in a harsh way, either. She
always told me real nicely. And that was enough
explanation for me.

Since there were no boys old enough to help
out in our family, my sisters and myself had to
do all the boys' chores. We didn't have any garbage dump at that time, so my duty was to go down
the beach every day and dump the garbage. That
was a job that the boys in other families did.
Cutting wood and splitting wood were other jobs
we had to do since the boys were too small. Even
when my two young brothers got older, my mom
pampered them. They didn't have to do those
chores. At that time I was resentful about it,
but now I say to myself, "Well, why should I have
felt like that? It was one of those things that
had to be." Now, I am kind of glad that I could
make things easier for my mom, because she tried
to make things easier for my dad.

In those days we didn't get our fruit like
people do now—go to the store. We couldn't.
We went out berry picking. Late September was

the time the cranberries would come out. We'd
cross the Sooyez River, and in a clearing was a
huge marsh. We wore boots into those marshes—
rubber boots that went over our knees, because
we were on our knees most of the time—picking.
The brush from the cranberries is real hard on
your hands, so we wore what I thought used to be
real cute—sock gloves. We all wore long black
socks then, and my mother would save them when
they had holes in them, and give them to my grandma. She would cut them up the heels and sew them
so they'd fit in between each finger. Then our
hands didn't get scratched too bad when we were
in the cranberry marsh. We'd put them on and the
ladies would pin them up close to our shoulders.
The only thing that got scratched up was the ends
of our fingers.

The mothers and grandmothers kept us pretty
close. We had to do our share of picking, but
had to babysit at the same time. I remember going to the cranberry marsh with one of my mom's
babies strapped on my back and another one attached
on one side of me, and I would pick with one hand.
My mother used both her hands since she didn't
have any babies with her. The women wanted to
get as much as possible, since berries were our
only fruit in the winter time.

Even though we worked a lot, we did have time
for fun. We liked being around boats, so often
we'd go out to the dock for entertainment. We'd
stand on the dock and ask the fishermen, "Can we
take care of your skiffs while you're on shore?"
Some of the nice ones would say, "All right, you
can take them; keep them until we get back."
Sometimes they'd be gone three, four hours, or
maybe half the day. So we'd be out there just
rowing away. We'd just play and ride the waves.
There wasn't any breakwater then and the waves
were big. We loved to ride the waves. Then,

when we wanted to go ashore we'd count waves, and
on the seventh one we'd just row like mad and come
in. I'd pull the skiff up on the beach and run
up and tell my mom I was hungry. Then later, I'd
pull the skiff back into the water and row to the
dock and check to see if the fisherman had come
back. Then I'd stay close around the dock in the
skiff and watch for him. I guess we learned how
to take those chances with the waves and paddle
the little skiffs. Our parents didn't seem to mind.
None of us ever drowned; we just learned how to
live with the ocean.

Our parents used to make spears for us, and
sometimes if it was pretty calm, we'd use the
skiffs to get flounders. They used to be here
in the bay before they built the breakwater. We
spent a lot of time doing that, and then when we
were finished, we'd wash the boat out and bring
it back to the fisherman. We took the flounder
we caught to the old people. They'd fillet it
or just cut it up and boil it. They used to
really enjoy it. These were some of the things
we used to do when we were kids in Neah Bay.

HELMA SWAN WARD
AND
LINDA J. GOODMAN

Severed Reality

It tightens the bonds
when you share with me.
An accidental meeting?
No, the Fates have
intervened.

At a hotel in
San Francisco, with
a waterfront view,
You were there—
as a candidate in
a big political campaign
with banners splashed
all over the lobby
bearing your face.

Then we were alone
on the deserted beach.
I said I wanted
to be on your left side
always close to your heart.
You told me
I always say
the nicest things.

Sometimes less is more.

FOSTINE B. TALLTREE

Spell for Resurrection

Bats flitter the twilit barn.
Thin cries of children,
  out to scare themselves
  with night-quickened hearts
summon the witching moon.

Trees,
  stripped to a winter coven,
read the bones of summer.
The year stirs in its sleep,
  covers its head with blankets,
  and chooses not to know what's going on.
Secret compartments hold the heart of children.
Once upon a time
ash, oak and thorn
sang them to sleep and silence.

They burst the wooden sides of their long dark
  and sing spring songs,
like colored flags
  pulled from the sleeves of angels
  who will not tell us how they do it.

They only give us a kiss
    and a key--
while children's voices sing spring songs
    in the quiet wood.

RUSTY NORTH

61

The Florida Book

This is outlaw country here in Miami.
Robert denied it at first and got very defensive. Everyone tries to hide. Privacy's the
thing. Big, big sprawled out ranch houses,
garages three cars wide. Huge lawns all around,
such a need for space. Not at all like New
England. Palm trees and fences, covering every
inch.

If I lived here, I would feed the doves and
the jays. I hear them humming. I smell fried
chicken again. Plane buzzing. The *er, er* sound
of some bird, cars whooshing back and forth on
the street. The sound of those big leafed rubber trees in the breeze. The faint sound of an
ambulance far away. It doesn't affect me here
in the sun, writing, shadows of trees caressing
my arms, the pool a vibrant turquoise. Lika
barks, I pull the towel up and over my breast.
I will start my period soon, it is full and ripe.

A lizard is walking face down, down the
trunk of the tree. It stops and holds on, its
body arched back. An orange sac billows out
from its throat with every breath.

A white lacy moth flitters in and out, its
wings like the fabric on my Easter Sunday dress
when I was 8. It was turquoise blue and had
raised pink bumps. I loved that dress. I might
have been a madonna wearing that dress.

I sit nude out here writing. I look around
for onlookers. I know I am taking a chance.
The lady next door was out yesterday in her big
straw hat thrashing through the plant nursery.
It's full of those jungle palms with flowers
that have huge pink velvet petals and 5 inch
stamens. Everything is so lush. All the avo-
cado pits I tried to grow in Connecticut would
flourish in Florida. I like the feeling of
growth and abundance, grapefruit dripping off
the trees; you'd never starve in winter.

I lay on my back and spread my legs to the sun. I wish the sun could penetrate me, warming the dark walls of my vagina. I stretch my legs wider apart until it feels like the sun has come inside, warming my cervix.

I grease my body up with sunblock. It is thick and the same color as motor oil. I am dying for a smoke—writing, coffee, sun, and cigarettes go hand in hand to me. So I hunt for the marijuana bag thinking inhaling a toke will dampen my craving.

Saturday.

I'm crying now. I kiss the dog on her muzzle. She doesn't know I'm leaving. Robert keeps asking me if I'm really going to leave today. He says I should call in sick.

I'm only going back because I couldn't stand their shock if I didn't return. I could tell them I want to live with my husband—lies—they think he lives in Ashford. I'm just waiting for the final days of the "jail term" to be over. I try to think of it like summer camp. Battered teachers, Nancy calls us.

At school I am babysitting 15 year old boys whose boredom and hyperactivity amaze me. I don't care if they are there, they don't care if they are there, we are only playing a game. I wonder if they know I'm lying. I tell them I want them to learn, but I really don't care.

My plane leaves tomorrow at 5:00 p.m. I am afraid. I am afraid I will quit writing. I am afraid I will become depressed.

*****

Eight Americans were killed in Iran yesterday. They were there to free the 53 hostages, but their equipment screwed up, and Carter cancelled the operation. As they were leaving, their planes collided. Eight airmen were killed and two were injured.

Last week, Mrs. Timm, mother of the young-
est American hostage, went to Iran to meet with
the Ayatollah to beg her son's release and to
see her son. They let her see him for 45 minutes.
Did they talk about relatives and the price of
hamburger? Was there a duck of his head, a
wince? Was he changed? Did he look like Howard
Hughes holed up in the attic of the Stardust?
Were there circles under his eyes? Did he shake?
How did she feel?

*****

A man in the Navy was found with his ear
sewn to his bed in Virginia.

*****

"In March, Frank Scheidell, an engineer fireman
for the USS Vreeland, charged that sailors removed his clothes, tied a rope around his ankles,
strung him upside down and greased his genitals."
4-25-80, *The Miami Herald*.

*****

A woman marathon runner came in first, beating her best time by one half hour. Experts say
it is impossible to improve that much. Would
they say that if a man had beaten his own record
by one half hour? I think she's honest (at
least my fingers are crossed).

*****

Linda Lovelace says she was coerced into
making *Deep Throat*. I believe her. I want to
write her and tell her I believe her. I will.

64

*****

Saturday 4-26-80 B727 Miami Airport
  Twelve days after Dad's birthday. My vacation is over. I sit nervous. My rings are off;
they trap my fingers. I am wearing my coach
clothes, my first class slit skirt's in the
suitcase.
  Even the stewardesses have messy perms now,
no more starched hairdos. Off the collar. A
woman's hair, her punishment, her bane. It must
not touch her clothing, that's all over now.
  The man on my right, across the aisle, asks
if he can read my paper. He says Carter shouldn't
have leaked the news that eight airmen were killed
in the Iranian desert after the rescue attempt.
He says he should have just ordered another raid.
"But it would nave leaked out sooner or later,"
I tell him. "Remember Watergate," he says. "It
would ruin Carter. If that didn't work out, they
should just go in and take over."
  I say, "We should give back the Shah, who
needs him?" He says, "If we do that then it
shows that Americans can be pushed around. If
we play into the hostage game, then everybody
will take hostages at the drop of a hat."
  He tells me that when the Shah was sick in
New York, they should have just pulled the plug
and given him back. I laugh, "It's a good idea."
"Don't think they didn't think about it," he says.
  We exchange newspapers. After reading his
for 12 minutes with a smokey headache, he asks
me, "Isn't it amazing how the two papers can
report the news so differently?" I have no idea
what he is talking about. They both seem the
same to me. I shake my head violently, yes.
Then I go ahead and read more of the paper, headache thrashing, to find articles to prove his
point.
  I find some references and I point out how
this newspaper says the U.S. should try another

65

rescue. He explains to me, then, how my paper
illustrates the scene with maps while his did
not.
I can't believe I went through all that.
I didn't even want to read his paper. He insisted.
It was five rows up, he had to borrow it back.
I think he has a headache, too. He's holding his temples. He takes two aspirin with selt-
zer.
I get out two aspirin, also, and swallow
them dry.
Before I spoke with this man, I thought he
might be kosher because he poked around his
chicken leg eating only his vegetables and salad.
No milk and dairy together. The chicken was
smothered under a melted slab of velveeta cheese.
He must think I am evil, I thought, requesting
milk to go with my meal.
Then after we started talking, I liked him,
although he looked like a man I used to write for
who fired me. He had his mouth, it was disturb-
ing. I saw his cold sterile thin lips. He has
a tight asshole, I used to think about him, his
perfect suits encasing him—his tailored shroud.

*****

Thank god for familiar faces. I see myself,
shaking, coming down off the airplane ramp, high
heels faltering. Thank god for Bridget. I will
smother her with kisses when I see her, she is
an extension, she knows who I am.
I can still see her playing M.C. at the con-
cert. As awkward as young Abe Lincoln, that's
what she looked like or like Gary Cooper, all
legs, slim hipped, nervous dimple, hands in
pockets.

*****

I want to call Jude, but I am afraid. Voice in
the wilderness. Pick up the phone. Everyone is
just a phone call away. I've called people up
out of the blue that I haven't spoken to in six
years. It's the shock I want of recognition.

*****

Willimantic, Connecticut, Sunday 4-27-80
    Bridget says she is getting frustrated
(slamming cupboards, looking for tea). "If there
aren't any teabags, I'm going to be upset," she
threatens. "What's your problem?" I say, defending myself. "There are definitely teabags."
    I am upset that she is frustrated, frustrat-
ed with me? I feel guilty—I shouldn't have ac-
cused her of having a problem. But then I think,
it's her problem, her frustration, why did I take
it on me? And all so instantaneously, defending
the teabags.
    Women, always making a fuss about their feel-
ings, give me a man who doesn't have any, it's
hard enough for me to deal with my own. That's
how Robert must feel when I talk about my feelings, defensive and guilty.
    I apologize for telling her she has a prob-
lem, "I'm sorry," the magic phrase that restores
everything proper. Not so, I learned the hard
way, grappling with words. I say,"I'm sorry
things got in such a mess," to Betsy, former
roommate, hoping I could restore the peace, but
there was nothing to restore. I never really
liked Betsy anyway. That bothers me, not being
able to be friends with her—we lived together
for a year, rooming, the perfect equalizer. We
speak to each other in guarded tones. She asks
me what I'm doing and about Robert. She doesn't
know I know she hates him; I don't trust her.
At least I got the phone number. The music is
too loud, it inundates me.

Maine vacation

I walked across the bridge at Boothbay Harbor, Maine, in the rain. It was a foot bridge, one quarter mile long, four feet wide, set on posts over the bay.

I passed a man about twenty-five years old. He walked fast. He had greasy, slicked back hair. He was walking with an adolescent German shepherd that yipped at me nervously. The man just walked real fast, determinedly, smoking hard on his cigarette. Soon as I got to the end of the bridge, a heavy, large-breasted, braless, shoeless woman wearing an old t-shirt stretched tight over her breasts shouted out at the figure already half way across the bridge, "Warren, don't you care about me? Don't you care about me at all?"

He probably couldn't hear her, what with the night sounds all around, but she kept walking, her face sad and sullen, shouting into the night.

JULIE ZANDER

Leaving Mexico City

We climb the berth to the sleeper and drop the
curtain. Wet fields of corn slosh by us, the dark
wedging closer pole to pole. The red wine hurts
your head and burns my bladder, but we like it.
We tear Oaxaca cheese to salt shreds to eat with
the bread. The apples you smuggled from the
States are delicious. Our bare feet touch, toe to
toe, while we feast.

The couple in the next berth are having an argument.
He is 20 years her senior, pink and pasty. They
had a baby this year. He can't sleep, doesn't like
her picnic of corn bread and chiles, and is mad that
she knows all the Spanish. We hear his sighs and
her spunky cough. When it is silent, we decide they
are kissing. We are all rocked too dizzy to sleep.

Mama rocked me this rough in Indiana when I napped.
She liked to bop-out to Cuban salsa music, clicked
her skilled fingers in my ears. I got my first motion
sickness on her lap, those flat lands of youth made
rugged by her knees. My early training prepared me
for this trip and I drift off with you in my arms.

I dream that we are back North building a cabin.
The couple in the next berth drive up in a pick-up
truck heaped with 2 by 4s. They remind us to add
on a nursery. When I wake up, you are picking the
bread crumbs from my hair and gazing tenderly at me.
Your eyes are the bright blue of the shawls at the
market, lit up like those wild and shy stars at our
window, the first stars we've touched on our journey.

RACHEL HERR

69

Cafe Life

Right here something is happening
here, where the great open straits
empty into bays
finger islands
become surrounded.

Here in the center of this water, these
islands
lowlands
one feels a prairie
ringed with mountains
spoken with wind skies
riding light's hours.

Here where the full pouch of the bay
curves the rising forest
drinks fresh streams
dreams long sand spits
breathes shallow muddy flats
yeasty with clams
rims rocks below

eagle aerie
cuts deep and winding coves
for heron, kingfisher
here convoluted and full
this bay can rise, fresh
unconfined
in the first wind.

In their cities
the dogs of pleasure, of culture,
of style
got word
they come and
keep coming
whining and yelping:
this is the place, something is happening,
this is the place.

They are right.
Outside the cafes the short bay
rises in winter's first winds and tides
begins to take back this
once sand bar, this now dog town.

RU KIRK

Humus

for Ernst

Fierce earth
rising
black eyed in the palms
is what you fear.
This groaning weight
would claim you
shuddering
in the bones planted
with desire before you
before any of us.
Black soil comes
stalking, shaking
out your life
last year's seed.
This wildness is not
woman/yourself
but the great fertile
breath
of season and tide
running
beneath our plans.

RU KIRK

The Passing of the Ohio

I woke early the other morning; rain gusts
rattled the skylight; gray was in the mirror and
outside in the high limbs a wind from somewhere
way out in the Pacific was all forlorn. Neither
siblings nor Mom were heard. They were gone to
Seattle for a few days' visit. No school. I
heard the fire door squeak downstairs, and Dad
rip the daily paper; drone and creaking of the
firebox as the heat came on. The lid rang as
the coffee pot hit the grill.

"Morning," Dad said as I climbed down the
ladder.

"Mornin'."

Water running off the roof splattered in
the plastic buckets; the river's spate seemed
to rise as the dawn grew.

"I saw where the U.S.S. Ohio is due to pass
through the Straits sometime right about now,"
he said.

"Oh," I thought, distantly, out loud, lifting a mug from a shelf. I could see that he was
pleased with the brisk blaze that the paper had
kindled and that the news was a joke, in a way.
His mood was inexplicably light for a morning
like this.

"Is that big nuke really going by, or what?"
I asked.

"I believe it," Dad said. "I read it in the
Times."

There was a long quiet. I've read and heard
some things about these new submarines, and from
how I felt this morning, the weather and event
seemed fitting.

There was another gust, the rain let off,
and it was silent.

Dad broke it, "What do you think? Can you
hear it?"

"I don't hear anything," I mumbled.

"Yeah, well that is kind of how those big

ones keep it," he said. "You can't hear them or
see them, but they are there."

I looked through the window at the shifting
gray masses. "They ascend from the deep like the
shark. You'd never know they were there to fear
except for that occasional sighting. Maybe we
should walk the beach and see if there are any
dark shadows in the waves. Maybe a tell-tale
ripple carried on the crest of the crashers?"

Dad laughed and poured himself a cup of coffee.

"You want to know what's made me scared?"
I asked.

Dad filled my cracked cup with coffee. We
sipped on the hot brew and I began my story.

"Remember McCloud-Ganga, the Tibetan refugee
camp? In Kashmir?"

Wet mists blot everything from sight and hush
the already quiet atmosphere. Only drops of fog
and maybe a low murmur of a chanter passing by
through the white can be discerned. At other
times bright sunlight filters between the tree
branches and brightens and renews the colors of
the intricately woven robes of the villagers,
all worn out with the travel of a wanderer. Sometimes the sun glances off the golden temples and
causes a shimmering haze in the street plaza where
the only shade is the Great Bo tree in the center
of the square.

Numerous paths honeycomb the slopes; they
are lined with carved boulders that generations
of people have shaped slowly, each placing a
stone here and a stone there to pace along while
they twirl their prayer wheels, count beads, and
chant. The colorful, triangular, religiously
inscribed flags they string between the trees and
from the steeples of their Buddhist temples give
a mystic air to that high region.

Speaking of temples! What places of tranquil

peace! After walking from the buzzing town
through the warm woods and the lovely temple
gardens, then stepping into these miniature
heavens, the beauty is overwhelming—great
vaulted edifices with cool, clean, stone floors
and polished wooden walls. Just sitting there
and hearing the continuous hum of monks praying
is enough temptation to fall asleep and never
have to see sorrow again. The ethereal peace
is shattered, though, by the sight of the awful
guardians. They stand sentinel, grimacing gro-
tesquely at passers of wanton intent. Masks
writhe; numerous bejewelled limbs with terrible
grips hold precious symbols aloft while clawed
toes rend and tear to pieces the mutable human
shape beneath them.

The horror of that human suffering filled
my mind with pain. I remember thinking, "Let's
get out of here!", after stepping from the sun
into the depths of the temple. I could hear the
flies outside, even the flies, humming mantras.
When my eyes adjusted to the dark I saw the huge
Golden Buddha, delicate features full of passive
pureness, wrought in gentle gold. Hope floods
back as sun streams into a dark room when the
shade is drawn from the window. I,for one,was
confounded and drawn into its sedateness.

"One day you informed me we were going for
a walk in the hills. I asked if I might not
stay and spend the time with Kathy. You agreed.
So, as you and Mom and baby sister disappeared
from sight, I ran off to my friend's home.
When I arrived, to my dread, her house was
vacant. You must understand that I was a
young child and had not been alone before.
Finally, when I knew I'd be unable to find her,
I sped home, terror and tears rising speedily
as a lump in my throat. Of course, you were
gone, but for some childish reason I had hoped

against all hope that you would be there to wrap
warm arms about my feeling of terrible loss. It
is hard to describe the forsaken and destitute
emotions that whirled through my innocent mind.
I even convinced myself that you hated me and
were never coming back.

"Gentle-faced people passed me, offering
solicitude at the sight of my tears but I saw
only monsters, like those guardians of Buddha's
temple, and shrank away. The peaceful Buddha
within did not appear. I couldn't even get in
the house (the door was locked) to hug and wrap
myself in one of Momma or Poppa's pieces of
clothing. At last I settled down on the door-
step prepared to die since my loved ones no
longer wanted me. There I fell asleep with dirty rivulets drying on my cheeks.

"And then you came back when the sun was
setting and found your poor abandoned baby on the
step," I concluded chuckling.

"I never knew that happened to you," Dad
mused laughing along with me. "Where was that
Buddha bud anyway?"

I set my mug on the table, stoked the fire
and went outside. I'd planned on going to work
right away, but it was raining so very hard, with
the trees all misty and the surf pounding away
monotonously to my right across the highway, and
I felt so sluggish that I just stepped back into
the house and Dad asked if I wanted any more coffee.

"Nah," I said. "I've already got the jitters.
But are you hungry yet? I'm not."

"I suppose I could probably wait awhile,"
he nodded.

A silence took hold as I leaned against the
wall in front of the fire and Dad stared off into
space. I could almost see his mind cranking away
behind his deeply creased face. The rain drummed

on the roof and the fire snapped and crackled
like rice crispies magnified.

"You know we were talking about India?"
I began. "Well, do you remember the time we were
on the Ganges?"

He nodded affirmatively.

"I really enjoyed the white sand, and how
every night the wind rose a little and washed
the pilgrim-trodden beach clean. The river was
grand too; deep blue in the middle and clear on the
edges, with all those logs floating down to the
mills. When we first were there, our home was
a cave pre-inhabited by the skeleton of an old
'Baba' who'd died there. Every morning we'd have
breakfast on the sand. But then you built that
rustic, river-log house. Then, when you were
barely done, those patrolers came floating down
on their inflated pigskins, making sure all of
the logs got to the mill. They ordered you to
disassemble the building in order for them to
retrieve their precious wood. You refused and
they kindly accomplished the task themselves.
Oh, well, the cave wasn't too bad.

"How about the time you and I were walking
to the village to buy some yogurt and you put a
holy cowpie on one of their shrines? Tin-Can Man
became angry at you and removed it. Remember the
Tin-Can Man? He was strange. He walked the dusty
paths every morning beating the sun up on an old
tin can and making a prodigious racket. But no
one stopped him so I guess it was all right.

"Even that guy, though, didn't spoil our fine
mood that morning. It was nice, though boiling,
with the sun burning down on the big leaved trees
and parched earth. The glinting river beckoned
sweaty, practically naked Hindus. We were enjoying
it just as much, for the long monsoon was over
and during that time there's about zilch sun."

The fire was getting low. I fed it. Dad lit

a cigarette and took up where I'd left off.

"Do you recollect when we were in the village and a 'Baba', painted all white, was in the street? He was chanting and attempting to transport himself on stubbed legs out of the milling, heedless crowd. I wonder what happened to him."

I recalled that memory only too well and it struck me as pitiful, all those striving people. We strive, too, but mostly for more capital and higher status. There they struggle for one more day of life.

"Yes, I remember him," I finally answered, feeling melancholy. "Somehow this morning all human strivings don't seem so different."

We contemplated my statement, harkening to incessant rain.

Dad broke the calm, "And those 'genteel' lepers by the bridge at Laxman Djula...."

"Ha, the beggars!"

And we laughed quietly together for "the beggars" brought back a hilarious scene.

Dad and I had left Mother and my little sister on the beach for a while to go across the river and visit a certain "Van Baba"; "Babas" were Indian hermits who dreamed away at the head of the Ganges and came only occasionally to the villages. When they did come, they were interesting to see and speak with. They were adept at the art of Yoga and were often mumbling prayers to Shiva; anyway, as we were coming back, Dad bought me a sack of peanuts to give the lepers who were friendly inhabitants of the bridge. When we reached them, I walked down their ranks doling out two peanuts to each, like a princess visiting her people. They cheered me on as we talked, after a fashion, as I knew little Hindi and they no English.

As I came to the end of the line and was about to give the last beggar his peanuts, I saw a huge monkey sitting by him. That area was covered

with free monkeys, some of them frightfully
ferocious. Just as I offered the gift to the poor
man, the monkey, unfortunately, saw that I had
over half a bag left, and quick as lightning, he
deprived me of my treasure, leaving only the torn
shreds of paper from the top of the bag.

At first I was shocked, but when I became
aware that he didn't plan to give it back and
was swiftly climbing the railings of the bridge
we were about to cross, I burst into tears. When
the beggars saw my plight, they leapt to their
feet, those who had feet, and began chucking lumps
of stone and laughing mock reproaches at the
creature, who sat there chewing peanuts and occasionally spitting shells and screeches at the
comically jerking humans below. They were amusing,
in a pathetic sort of way, for it is difficult to
pick things up when your hands and fingers have
been eaten away by disease. If I'd been older,
the sight of these forlorn folk getting a laugh
out of such a small incident, would have made me
brood; but at the time, I only burst into laughter.

I shifted my position and noticed the rain
had stopped.

Dad said, "Well, you know now, they were
putting on a show for their princess."

"Yes, I guess so," I mused.

I glanced at the clock. "I guess I'll get
going," I smiled indicating the time.

He sighed, "I think I'll go down and look
for shadows of the passing Ohio in the waves."

I poured steaming water into the bowl for
dishes.

ARYANA BATES

Excerpts

The process of talent. One doesn't *become* an actor or a writer or a sculptor or whatever but is always *becoming*. One is what one is until the end, whether or not always visibly *producing*. The process defines the identity of the artist more than does the product.

Most of us will work our whole lives, sometimes turning out a good piece, usually *not*, usually just managing to make adjustments and compromises to keep the talent together, keep it fueled, just managing to keep struggling with the consequences of a talent, the responsibilities it implies.

Most of us don't have a talent big enough to sustain us daily, hourly, moment to moment. There are great, gaping days of darkness between the bursts of light.

And in the end, there's no promise that the talent is a *talent*, and not a compulsion of some other less blessed sort/source.

Believing in one's talent, as believing in God, requires a leap of faith.

*****

I am not being a good mother today. I am impatient and short with Renata. I'm not letting her be three years old. I'm not being a good wife today. I'm sullen and falsely apologetic and truly close-mouthed. I'm not being a good person today. I am weak and unforgiving. *Mea culpa, mea culpa, mea maxima culpa.*

*****

Sins of omission and sins of commission are equal. "We have left undone those things which we ought to have done, and we have done those things which we ought not to have done; and there is not health in us."

*****

Today is a mostly wonderful day despite fierce winds and a lashing, rainy coldness. Mostly wonderful because Renata and I spent the day at the bicycle races. Strength, bright colors, the whirr of spokes and speed. The bulging clusters of muscle above the racers' knees.

Pumping up the Washington Street hill, away from us, the racers are a cluster of bobbing helmets and black bottoms. Their legs, from a distance, more like tiny wings than pistons, like a hundred hummingbirds, a miracle of motion.

They are a collective testament to the beauty of self-discipline, and the many possibilities implied by and inherent in discipline. Self-discipline is an artistic statement expressing self-respect.

*****

I can't sustain it. Everything crumbles, falls apart, fades.

*****

When I was younger, when I was in high school and college, I was satisfied being full of the immediate business of living. Then, the immediate business of living was *learning* (i.e. reading and writing and acting). Now the immediate business of living is making money for food and shelter and clothing.

I spent the first years of my life learning, and now the demands of daily living seem bent on squelching that impulse.

*****

I need a measurable triumph. I need to

82

accomplish something tangible beyond being A
Good Waitress at work, beyond attending to the
consuming tiny tasks required by my family and me.

My self-esteem dwindles, my confidence is
fragile, my expectations diminish. My creativity
is splintered and its fragments are too small to
cut through the night, but array themselves like
distant stars in the darkness.

I'm not at all certain that my moderate gifts
will necessarily survive this period of atrophy.
It seems altogether too possible that they will
be abused and ignored to death. I have seen it
happen. Talents wither. Gifts fall victim to
poor stewardship as regularly and tragically as
other natural resources.

I don't believe a talent will endure unless
it is honored. Can it be honored in the breach?

*****

I spend more time in this journal and on
letters than I do on any story-telling. I wish
I could just leave myself alone, get myself off
the page and get on with my writing.

And I don't even like myself much, these
days. These days are cluttered with nothing, and
I am too full of myself and my habits to attend
to myself by forgetting myself altogether.

I do forget that these phases and stages of
life are transitory, so I think this devolution
will continue endlessly, and I fret and moan about
it. I forget that there will be a turning-around
time, a gathering together, and this unravelling
will cease.

*****

I can't write today, I just can't write. I can
barely think.

*****

(Later)
I can't even think.

*****

    As a writer, I am my own witness insofar as
I exist in relation to the past; the present me
is a witness to me as I was, is a witness of me
as I am (which immediately becomes the past). I
am at once the do-er, the one who watches the do-er
and the one who writes down what the do-er did and
how the watcher watched, and also how the writer
writes about how the watcher watched and how the
do-er did. But, in point of fact, the writer *is*
the watcher, *is* the do-er. (The concept of the
Trinity was never hard for me to grasp.) The
writer writes about watching watching and watching
doing and watching writing.
    (This is part of why I am a good actress, I
am accustomed to living with more than one pair
of eyes.)

*****

    Me and my petty writer's tribulations.
    I think of the victims and martyrs of the
world and know I'm morally obligated to justify
my presence. I must take responsibility not only
for my own little life, but also for my own little
life among others. My *vita activa.* I must justify
the food and air and water I consume and the waste
I produce.
    Being a witness is not enough.
    I know of the presence of the *desaparecida,*
I know of the children of war, I know of the a-
trocities performed on husbands and daughters and
lovers, atrocities performed by husbands and daughters and lovers.

84

By not doing enough I am party to their
slaughter.
And I never do enough. I am never enough.
How can I live with that knowledge?

*****

Of those of us who have witnessed a death,
who can forget the sound of life leaving the
body after the noisy violence of man and nature
has been done, who can forget that gentle, sudden
sound, the small end of the final breath?

*****

I am too weak to be anything but a writer.
The witness.
I feel my infinitesimal insignificance within an immense and disinterested universe. I don't
believe in any power greater than the random energy
of the universe. If there was once a benevolent
God watching over us, he has abandoned us by now.
I cling, however, to any fragment of evidence
to the contrary.

*****

There is a small piece of moon tonight and
a large, loud wind. I drink retsina and listen,
look. I can't see beyond my own reflection in
the window, the darkness is so dark out there
and the light in here is bright.
I ponder matters of light and darkness—
symbolic and otherwise—during these days of
Advent. (The rituals and liturgy of the church
are an unconscious part of me; I think it will
be so until I die, whether or not I ever go to
church again.) Advent will always be for me a
season of prayer and fasting.
"Cast away the works of darkness and put
upon us the armor of light."

Looking out the window tonight Renata chanted,
"Star that I see, I wish for me."
If I could sing a song now, sing a song new
to the earth and sky, I'd sing to you, Renata, I'd
sing to you.

*****

Practicing the piano again is good for me;
these months we've had the piano, I've played almost every day. And because of this small atten-
tiveness and concentration, I improve.
(Such is not the case with daily writing; I
don't have the assurance that I'm getting better.)
Mostly working on *The Well-Tempered Clavier*
which will occupy me for the rest of my life, I
suspect. I like the present but invisible passion
of Bach's keyboard works.

*****

How I miss acting. I miss mostly, I think,
the communal act of acting. I miss listening to
the other actors, the other characters, and building with them a new creation.
With writing, it's altogether different. I
have to listen to the sounds of memory, because surrounding me and this typewriter is silence.
The beauty of writing, and its pain, is that
it is solitary, solitary, solitary.

ROBIN BIFFLE

Reluctant Muse

Looking at myself: I am poet, painter, piano
player, molder of clay, divided as night from
day. No grays of dawn or twilight, no softened
blues, no rosy hues warm the cold of limited
sight, but day and night.

An artist? Of what I am not sure for locked
within this facade that isn't really me at all
is music still-born or unplayed, breathtaking
unpainted beauty mushrooming inside. Words written without a pen tossed aside in mind, again,
at night. Not day, but night.

A canvas bare becomes a mountain peak, a quiet
creek reflecting flowering trees and a building,
old with water rot, mirrored in a dammed-up pond.
The pond now swells, cascades, and rushes on
toward darkening sky. Bypassing twilight, I am
a person of that night.

A block of clay is scraped away into a form. I've
caught a trace but not enough resemblance there.
I pinch and pat and pound away all hours day and
night. But still, I cannot get it right...not
day or night.

A piano that I loved to touch played not much the
music that dwelled and swelled within. Ejects
dejected harmony, songs simplified, not quite ob-
scuring inability, I fortissimo away, a person
lost to day.

When will my day come for a mixed-up me? With
music that flows hesitatingly? From inept fingers
stained with paint that tried but failed to capture pictures of a saint? Or, with talent small,
bleeds words or births a statue incomplete? When
will this dark of night leave me for light of day?

"So what!" if I become a lesser luminary. At least I tried. In my own home my words and works all hang with family pride. So now I say, "I'll play my music anyway. What matter that it is the night or day!"

PHYLLIS MUSE MILLER

The Red Lodge

One day, out of a storm, a woman wearing uncomfortable clothes walked into the Learning Lodge. She met and spoke with the People she had never met before and yet had known for a long, long time. She sought aid from them from the perils of the storm. Being she was a guest, the People clothed her in warm blankets and fed her good food which warmed her heart and mind. Slowly came her strength.

After a short stay, she asked, "Father and Mother, I am seeking the path of enlightenment. Will you help me find it?"

The People talked amongst themselves for a while.

"Daughter," they said, "if you truly seek this path, you must start your search at the Red Lodge of the South for all journeys start and end there."

"I will go!" she said.

After three days of walking, she became very tired and her mind began to wander here and there looking for the easier path. The more her mind wandered, the more tired she became. Finally, she ṣlumped under a large cedar tree to rest, and started to fall asleep.

"Little Sister, Little Sister," a voice called. "Little Sister, Little Sister, up here!"

The woman was startled and shaking.

"Little Sister," the voice called, "Look up."

In the tree sat three owls, a black one, a white one, and a yellow one.

"We have been waiting for you," the owls said.

"You knew I was coming?" Little Sister asked.

"Of course," said White Owl. "We have always known!"

"Ho! Then you can help me find the Red Lodge," said Little Sister with relief.

"Oh, Little Sister! That is not for us to

find, that is for you alone to find," said White
Owl. "We are here to help you remember."

With that, Little Sister watched Black Owl
land on a fallen tree across from her, and change
into a beautiful young woman in a soft white
buckskin dress and moccasins. Yellow Owl then
landed next to Young Woman and changed into an
elderly woman with long white braids that lay on
the ground. Little Sister recognized them immediately. She ran and embraced them laughing
and crying at the same time. They all began to
talk at once. After a while, Grandmother spoke.
    "It is good you have come to us. We have
kept you in our hearts. There is much work to
do. We must start."
    "Yes!" agreed Young Woman. "Now that we are
one, and always have been, and always will be,
we must rest for the journey is long tomorrow."
    They all laid down in each other's arms and
went to sleep while White Owl watched over them.
So ended the First Day and it was good.
    As Grandfather Sun started his daily journey,
Little Sister awoke alone yet full. She smudged
herself and performed the Sacred Platform for
she now desired to approach each day in a sacred
manner. She collected food from Mother Earth,
thanked Her for Her give-away, and ate. Remembering the meeting of the night, she started on
her way. She listened to the songs of the birds,
songs of the trees, and began to recognize her
own song was a part of the music of the day.
As she walked, she felt as though she was directed—
being called as it were—yet she knew not from
where this feeling came, nor where it was leading
her. And yet, she followed.
    Towards evening, a dark cloud came overhead
and seemed to muffle the earth. Her song grew
quieter and quieter. She felt the need for pro-

tection from the coming storm. She made a shelter of pine boughs and a fire to warm her. The storm raged, blowing dust in snorts, pulling out bushes and trees. Again Little Sister's fears overtook her. For two days, she lay in her shelter and quaked, listening to the high shrieks of lightning and the deep, strong bellows of thunder around her. She hoped the fight would soon be over, and as she hoped, she slept.

When she awoke, Grandfather Sun was high in the sky. She felt the need to hurry so she dressed quickly, returned her shelter to Mother Earth, approached her day, and started on her way. Soon she came to a river, and sat down to rest.

"Little Sister, Little Sister, up here!"

Little Sister looked but could not see.

"Little Sister, look hard! I am up here."

Finally Black Bird flew down and landed on a rock near her.

"Boy! Whew! That girl ain't got a lick of sense!" the bird fussed. "You call her and you call her and she still can't see. I have a friend who needs your help now! Come on."

With that, Black Bird turned into a tumbleweed, and rolled along the ground to the west. Unsure, Little Sister followed slowly, keeping the tumbleweed in sight. It rolled to a clearing near the river and stopped. Beside it lay a raccoon that had been killed by the storm. Little Sister was filled with feelings, rolling powerfully through her—anger, pity, shame, fear, joy, and purpose all at the same time. Her heart began to cry. She knew and yet did not know, and the clouds within her grew. She heard a voice.

"It must be skinned and returned to Mother Earth in a sacred manner."

The voice came from the tumble weed. As Little Sister watched, the tumbleweed turned

into a tall, handsome young warrior holding a
large knife.

"She must be returned to Mother Earth in
a sacred manner," he said again.

"Teach me and I will help," responded Little
Sister.

As they skinned and prepared Raccoon, many
thoughts passed through Little Sister. Thoughts
of life and death and their dance of balance,
thoughts of the ones who have passed on to the
spirit world, and the ones still traveling the
path to the Great Spirit, thoughts of love and
living, all rushed through her and around her.
She saw them dance. After praying and returning Raccoon to Grandmother Earth, the young
warrior turned to Little Sister.

"My name is One Who Listens To The Wind.
You have learned much today. Take it to your
heart. It is your friend as I am. When you
need help, become quiet and learn to listen to
the wind. It will guide you. Here is a present from Raccoon to help you on your journey."

He handed her the right paw of Raccoon. He,
then, did a cartwheel or two, turned into a
tumbleweed, and rolled away towards the west.
Shortly, she saw a black bird circling overhead.

She took the present of the paw, and the
warrior's words to her heart, and understood.
She made camp there by the river that night and
warmed her mind with the teachings of the day.

So ended the Second Day and it was good.

Little Sister crossed the roaring river with
the wind at her back and her song in her heart.
She walked along and chatted with her friends,
the trees, the winged ones, and the four-leggeds
that scurried along beside her.

Rounding a bend, she saw a clearing in the
trees. In the glade sat a sweat lodge. Beside
the sweat lodge stood a beautiful deer, soft and
brown, waiting for her.

"Little Sister, you must gather the rock people. They will tell you how," said the deer. "Little Sister, go now!"

Little Sister looked and looked, but the rock people hid from her. She returned to the deer.

"Deer, the rock people have no words for me, and I know not how to talk with them," cried Little Sister.

"Little friend, rock people talk only to ones who prepare themselves to listen. Smoke your pipe for the Great Spirit to open your heart and your ears."

Little Sister followed the words of her guide and became still. She smoked four times, thinking and praying to the fire people, the wood people, the rock people, and the water people, and to her journey. Slowly, she was filled. She arose and found that darkness was close. She searched and found a rock. She reached out for it and it spoke softly.

"I am not one!"

She continued to search and found another.

"Yes, Little Sister, I am one!"

She gave away tobacco, and gently picked up the rock. So in this manner, she gathered thirty-six rock people to hold the energy while she prayed in the sweat.

When the sun came up, Little Sister used the teaching of the wind to gather wood, sage, and cedar. After her collecting was done, she sat again and smudged and smoked for aid from the Great Spirit. Darkness and the full moon came as she made the fire for the rock people. She heard the rustle of winged ones land in the trees to the north of the clearing. She sang her song to them.

As she sang, her sisters slowly appeared and

said, "Little Sister, you journey long and learn much. We are always with you. Now is time and always now. Know your name in your heart. Your heart beats as one with all. Know your brothers and sisters. You, Owl Song, are growing. Now is the time to flower. Sweat and receive that which is from and of all worlds and from the One Mystery."

Little Sister took her name with heart, and entered the *inipi* ceremony. At the first door, she opened her mind to all the fears and perils in her heart. At the second door, she named and became one with her brothers and sisters, the rock people, the plant people, the four-leg-geds, the winged ones, Grandfather Sun, and Grand-Mother Earth—all the Peoples. At the third door, she gave away all thoughts, energies, all. At the fourth door, she entered the hum of silence of the Great Spirit, and saw and heard the wheel. The family sang and danced for her, with her, for all.

Leaving the sweat lodge, Owl Song saw all—children, friends, ancestors of the past and future. The clearing was filled with spirits as far as was known and seen. And surrounding them all was the Red Lodge of the South as it always has been and ever will be.

After the dancing and singing—with the moon still high and full—Owl Song slept with her family, snuggled close to keep her warm for the journey was long and the path was new.

So ended the Third Day and it was good.

Owl Song awoke to the calling of the wind, gently pulling her from sleep.

"Owl Song! Awake!"

She turned in the direction of the voice to find the large white owl she had come so well to know, sitting close by. White Owl looked deeply into Owl Song's eyes and heart, for a long time. Slowly White Owl changed into an old, old woman with so many wrinkles, she looked like the bark of an old tree. A voice, like the rustle of leaves said, "Come, Daughter, sit and talk. You have seen the Red Lodge. What did you see?"

"Old One, I saw the First Law, that every thing is born of woman, the receptive cup of creation. I learned we must hold and honor that energy always. I saw the active liquid movement of conception. I learned love is the energy of all movement on this earth and every-where. Every rock, tree, animal, bird, and person is born of that conception, and therefore we are all one. We are all her children!"

"Ho! My child, you have done well. Now, prepare yourself to go. Plan carefully for your work is hard and the journey is long."

Owl Song looked frustrated and confused, and began to protest.

"Old One, I just got here. I have sought long and hard for my family. I want to stay with them a while. I want to celebrate my..."

Owl Song stopped short and sat down slowly. Gathering around the Old One was the family that was, is, and ever will be. Her sisters, her brothers, the winged ones, the four-leggeds, the plants, the rocks—all of them. Again, the teaching of the sweat lodge flowed through her. She started to cry and sing and pray. As she did so, all gathered there came to her and touched her, one by one. This took three days and nights. She grew to know her/their world, her/their feel, her/their past, her/their future. She grew to know again her oneness with each and of us all. When this was done, Owl Song sat quietly, open, receptive, and traveling the Rainbow Bridge of peace.

Finally Old One spoke.

"You see, Owl Song. Seeing the Red Lodge of Trust and Innocence is just the birth of oneness in each of us. There is the Black Lodge of Introspection and Intuition, the White Lodge of Wisdom and Logic, and the Yellow Lodge of Illumination and Enlightenment. The journey to each of these carries many births and deaths, many beginnings and endings, and all are long and hard. All are necessary. Each holds a teaching. That is the Rainbow Bridge of Peace. They are held by the First Law—everything is born of woman! Holding this Law in our hearts, we walk the Law of the Earth to life. Do you know that Law now?"

"Yes, Old One. Do nothing to harm the children! We are all her children! I am ready to walk the Rainbow Bridge."

As Owl Song spoke, the Old One changed into White Owl and was joined by Black Owl and Yellow Owl.

"Know we are always with you," they said. Off they flew, singing the owl's song.

So ended the Fourth Day and it was good.

KAREN WILKS

Climbing

"Don't climb on that, you'll fall!" "Step back from there, you'll fall!" "Girls don't climb trees, get down or you'll fall!" Eventually...dreams and nightmares, always falling through space, off buildings, off mountains...waking just before I landed, but waking drenched in sweat, my heart pounding and remembering the fear and terror in-stilled since childhood...

I was terrified now, wet and muddy since the point I had slipped on the trail, but not yet cold. The sweat was still warm on my overheated body.... And now I felt the fear! Someone had just said, "This is it!" I looked up until the rain was splashing fully on my upturned face. I was stand-ing on a narrow shelf looking directly at a solid rock face on Green Mountain that seemed to reach up forever into the cloudy sky. I was there to climb that cliff and this was our final practice before climbing real mountains....

Suddenly, my reasons for being there seemed stupid and foolish; I knew I couldn't climb that cliff...I knew I would fall and could feel, even as I stood there, the endless tumble of my body through empty space. I thought of the dry, warm house I had left that morning after squirming into the many layers of clothes required for this "fun" sport, and forcing my feet into new, heavy climb-ing boots that required obvious effort with each step. Finally, at the trailhead, strapping on my backpack filled with 40 pounds of necessities. All this effort to go into a storm where the rain fell so hard, it splashed back as each wind-driven drop struck the ground...To climb a narrow trail overshadowed by rain-soaked brush that unloaded its water-laden leaves onto the one area of cloth-ing that the rain had been unable to reach. Be-tween jacket and gaiters, my wool pants were now sodden and heavy with water. After muttering,

99

"You've got to be kidding!" I shut my mouth and tried to look like any other student in the class... casual and nonchalant.

My mountaineering class numbered about thirty, including the rope-leader/instructors, ranging in age from eighteen to their mid-fifties. Other than myself at 34, the other lone female was in her mid-twenties, and the few other women were wives of the climbers.

Slowly I unstrapped the waist buckle to my backpack and gratefully shrugged my arms free, then propped my pack out of the way against some brush. We gathered together, huddled against the driving rain, and listened to instructions. We would have to make eight different ascents, each on a succeedingly harder route. Nothing was really different from what we had already learned but this was for real. The first student climbers would be belayed by the rope leaders until they made the ascent. Then the rope leaders would supervise while the students belayed the next group. These in turn would belay the third group while the first student group rappelled back down the cliff to make another ascent, a tougher one....

Correct terminology would be used at all times. "Falling!" screamed through my mind and continued its echo....

I watched the rope leaders free climb up the cliff carrying the ropes, finding hand and foot-holds in places I couldn't see, and looking like spiders scurrying up a web. Almost immobilized by now with fear, I stepped back to let the others line up to be first, my mind screaming, "I can't, I can't!"

Too soon, it was my turn. I hadn't had a heart attack or a stroke, so there was no way now to avoid climbing except to just walk away... and I couldn't do that and keep living in my skin. After all, wasn't this why I was here...to conquer an ever-increasing fear of heights and falling?

Of course it was! I thought back to what I had
already learned about myself in this class. Hadn't
I survived a night in a snow cave I had helped
dig out on the slopes at Mount Rainier? Hadn't I
mastered the Prusik knot and learned to enjoy
climbing up and down a climbing rope with it?
Sure I had! The snow cave might even have been
enjoyable if I had been with a very close friend...!

I knew that there was no way to get hurt here.
Slings, bowline knots, everything was checked and
double-ckecked. Finally, roped up and shaking, I
managed to squeak out "Climbing!" in response to
repeated calls of "Belay on!" "Climb!" echoed
down faintly and I started up. My boots slipped
in the slimy mud as I groped for handholds and
places to put my toes. Slowly I inched my body
upward, feeling the rock with wet, cold fingers...
sometimes hanging on with just my fingertips
until I could reach for a better handhold.

Suddenly my left arm flailed in vain for a
new hold in the rock! Nothing! Nowhere to go...
I was stuck...! I couldn't find even a tiny crack
to use! I looked down, far beyond the narrow
ledge from which I had started, and froze, yell-
ing, "Tension...!" The rope tightened around my
waist and I felt a little more secure. I yelled
up that I was stuck and soon heard a voice telling
me to reach for a crack above and to the left of
my head. Without panic this time, I waved my
hand around until my fingers felt the rough crack.
Jamming my hand in and curling my fingers to make
that hold secure, I climbed on. Each time I got
stuck that same voice would tell me where to find
a new hold and get me moving again.

Finally...the top! I crawled up over the
edge until I could get my shaking legs underneath
myself and stand up. The "voice" helped me all
through the rest of that long day, every time I
"froze."

Mount Washington was one of the most memorable climbs I made with my class that year because of the unusually heavy snowfall. I made it to the peak and felt again the thrill and exhilaration of making the summit. The panorama of the other snow-covered mountains and the pure pristine beauty helped slow the beating of my heart.

After lunch, the descent. These were usually easy for me. Midway down though, we came to a relatively smooth, snow-covered slope that seemed to stretch out forever below us. Suddenly, I felt the old fear, and started to turn toward the mountain to begin creeping down backwards when someone shouted, "No! We go down this way!"

"This way" looked crazy to me. Everyone was leaping out into space with gigantic steps, sinking into the snow, then leaping out again. I watched for only a moment, then gripped my ice ax, faced straight out and started stepping down the mountain. Sinking into the snow and briefly wishing for longer legs, I struggled to lift each successive leg up and out of the snow for the next step, forgetting all about falling in the fight to just move. The way I was lifting my legs out and then down reminded me of watching male dogs next to a favorite tree, so I started leaping like the others. When leaping, the snow didn't have a chance to grip my legs again and I experienced ever-increasing glee as I plunged down the mountain. It was exhilarating, like flying! A bit more work than glissading, but fun....

Later, riding home on the bus, I thought about the brief moments when I had felt perfect harmony between mind and body, and I wanted more of those moments. I was learning how to handle myself in unusual situations and was finding that I didn't always have to think throughout an exercise about what to do next. The mind and body would just work together.

SHARON M. O'HARA

An Introduction to Marian Taylor

I knew there was a special magic about Marian Taylor long before I knew who she was or had the good fortune to meet her.

Actually, it was her home that had captured my imagination. During my travels for a social service agency several years ago, my supervisor/friend, Candace Hulbert and I would take the Old Blyn highway as a respite from the fast-paced traffic on 101. Candace pointed out an old clapboard farmhouse, painted white with a dark green trim and set back from the road, snuggled up against a hillside, next to the picturesque railroad tracks. We often fantasized about who lived there and how. Somehow we pictured the house's occupants in the female and the singular. She was an older woman, a vibrant grandmother, we imagined.

So, when Helen Shaw, Vista Volunteer for her Jamestown Clallam tribe, suggested I contact a certain Marian Taylor in my search for writings for this anthology, and I did, Marian gave me directions that rang a bell. Sure enough, when I pulled into the drive, it was *the* house and the imagined occupant took on real flesh. A vibrant grandmother would be just one way to describe Marian Taylor.

She graduated in 1927 from the University of Washington's School of Journalism and that same day married her fiance of three years, Fred Taylor. She and Fred settled into a long and fruitful partnership, raising three children and eventually running an oil distributorship together. Marian also worked almost twenty years as a caseworker for the Department of Social and Health Services, the last eight as a medical caseworker for West End tribes.

Because Marian put herself through school by waiting tables at the University Faculty Club

and by staffing the reserve desk at the library,
she was unable to work on the college newspaper
and couldn't graduate with honors as a result.
Her only direct use of her journalism degree was
during her involvement with *The Sequim Press* in
the 1950's, what eventually became the current
Jimmy Come Lately Gazette.

Marian is of Jamestown Clallam, Swedish and
Irish descent and learned early to honor her
Native heritage. Her mother, Mary Ann Lambert
Vincent, wrote several historical pieces about
the tribes in the area, including *A Geneological
Story of the Olympic Peninsula Clallam Indians,
The Seven Brothers of the House of Ste-tee-thlum,*
and *The Dungeness Massacre and Other Regional Tales.*
Marian recalls her Clallam grandmother with loving
fondness and has translated her heritage into an
"Indian" room, filled with carefully kept journals
and other artifacts. She is always willing to
take the curious visitor on a tour through the
small, but treasure-filled room, and shortly before I visited her, had opened her home to an
elementary school class, generously sharing her
time and knowledge with them, as she did with me
several times.

Presently, Marian is on the Tribal Housing
Committee and has been an active member of the
Tribal Council in the past.

During my first visit with Marian, we circled
around and around the possible topics she could
write about, and as I began to get ready to leave,
she blurted out her desire to "do" the "Pack Train
Grandmother" article, which follows, from a 60
year perspective. Eventually, her story arrived,
along with the true tale of "Seam-Itza," a precious
gleaning from Marian's files.

CHRISTINA V. PACOSZ

Pack Train Grandmother

"Grandma, did you really own a little bear?" asked Danielle.

"Could you really ride a horse and shoot a gun?" asked Lindsay.

My two granddaughters and I were looking at some of my old mountain pictures. When I answered yes, the two little girls were excited and quite impressed.

"Tell us about it and how come you had a bear anyway," they asked. So here's the story.

When I was fourteen my mother married Frank Vincent, veteran guide and packer in the Olympics. His territory was the Dosewallips River country. Why me instead of my brother when he picked a helper? I'm not sure that I definitely was the more interested. At the age of ten I had been given a copy of *Tarzan of the Apes* for Christmas and from that time had tried to emulate him. I didn't want to be Jane, I wanted to be like Tarzan. Many a young fir tree bore wounds caused by my efforts to swing from limb to limb. No matter that Washington firs were not made for swinging, I tried. Perhaps I had succeeded to some extent and perhaps Frank saw the Tarzan in me and made his choice.

Frank taught me to ride and shoot and throw a diamond hitch over a loaded packhorse. An affinity developed between the horses and me. The Dosewallips was Frank's country and soon became mine too. It has been many years since I rode the trail, but I still feel that it is my country.

In the spring and summer we packed in supplies for the Forest Service, back-to-nature folks, artists, photographers, botanists, sightseers and an occasional prospector. In the fall we packed in hunters and brought out their game. I was going to high school at this time but was allowed to take the hunting season off. Some

of the boys griped about this but Mr. Davis told
them that when they "got straight A's as Marian
does" they could have the hunting season off, too.

The horses were pastured at our home in Blyn
in the winter months, and in the spring we would
wrangle them from Blyn to the river, where our
summer base was the Archer place a few miles a-
bove the Corrigenda Ranger Station. It would be
impossible to drive a dozen horses over the highway now, but this was in the early 1920s and
there was comparatively little traffic. Our lead
horse was a gray mare named Nellie. She wore a
bell on these trips and most of the horses followed her lead without any trouble. Once in a
while an untrained youngster might try to turn
off into greener pastures or an unfenced back
yard. A few times I did this herding job without Frank and with only a young boy for help.
Once as we were going through Quilcene a group
of children ran after us calling, "Come out
everybody, see the gypsies."

The first trip up in the spring was hard
work but exciting. In places the trail was
washed out from the winter snows. Forest Service
lines were down and trees were across the trail.
Worst of all were the yellow-jackets who had
built their nests in the muddy trail. A yellow-
jacket at any time is not a friendly creature,
but when a dozen or so horses have walked over
their homes, they come out stinging. I always
rode the last horse in the string to keep any
stragglers moving. Often I rode Carrots, a
rugged individualist. Where the other horses
would take off bucking and kicking, Carrots would
stop still in the trail and try to bite the yellow devils that were in his fetlocks. After
about two such incidents I learned to hold Carrots
back until the other horses had gone through,
then away we went in a mad gallop, risking

decapitation from dangling telephone wires.

On this first trip we usually packed in Forest Service supplies, fixed the trail, took out the fallen trees and, in some instances, were able to fix the telephone line which was a single wire attached to trees. Frank had a sort of gentleman's agreement with the rangers. When we were on the trail, we would report any potential trouble spots that we could not take care of. If all was clear, they were saved an unnecessary long hike. In return they would let us know if the game warden was on the prowl. It had been understood for a long time that Frank could have "camp meat," but there had been a disagreement with the current game warden. The privilege had been withdrawn and now there was sort of a contest between the two. We were always at risk.

Once as we were packing out, the ranger called and told us that the game warden was waiting at Corrigenda and that he was planning us no good. We did have camp meat and Frank had no intention of leaving it behind to spoil. Besides, he could not ignore the challenge. A mile above Corrigenda, Frank took the meat off the horse and draped it over my arm, then threw my jacket over the meat. When we got to the ranger station, the warden was waiting and carefully searched every pack. He was almost apoplectic when he found nothing and Frank thanked him for unpacking the horses for us. We went safely on our way but I had a sore arm for days from the weight of the venison.

The Dosewallips country has its legends, although in all our years in the mountains we never saw a sign of Big Foot. At one spot below Camp Marian, if one is quiet, he or she might hear the chopping of a woodcutter who was lost in the hills and is still trying to chop his way out. Happy Camp, just below Muscott Ranger

Station, was named by a man who went into the hills to try to cure his tuberculosis. Successful, he named the spot Happy Camp.

Perhaps the best known tale is that of a Mr. Muscott, for whom the ranger station was named. The story goes that Muscott, a Seattle man, found gold up the river and, understandably, would not reveal its source to anyone. He would go into the hills, hiding his trail, stay in the hills a week or two and return home, his supply renewed. Then, when this ran low, up he would go again. Many people tried to follow him, but he was always able to elude them. He could be followed as far as Happy Camp and then would disappear in the rocks. One fellow was persistent, trailing him again and again but always losing him at Happy Camp. One day Muscott, who probably thought he had outdistanced all of his pursuers, was drinking from the river when he was shot. The "tracker" was arrested and charged with murder. The jury was convinced from his testimony that he thought he was shooting at a cougar, and he was acquitted. His story probably was true because with Muscott dead no one ever has been able to find his gold.

About four miles below Dose Meadows Ranger Station, Frank built a woodsman's dream of a cabin to be used as an upper base for our packing operation. He named the camp after me, Camp Marian. My mother's name also was Marion, spelled with an o, but he made it clear that it was named after me. A few years ago I was told rather haughtily by a ranger's wife that the Park Service and the Forest Service do not name stations after living people. When Frank built the cabin, he had a ninety-nine year lease on the property which at that time was a part of the Roosevelt Monument. When the Monument became part of the Olympic National Park, it was closed to hunting.

This took away the largest part of our income from the pack train, and the property was allowed to revert back to the government. The name stuck and although the cabin long since has disappeared it still gives me a thrill to see "Camp Marian" on some old Forest Service map.

Frank was always sure I could do anything he wanted me to. No horse ever had been ridden to the top of Mount Sentinel, so I rode Badger, Frank's saddle horse, to the top of Mount Sentinel. No horse had ever been ridden down the steep slope of Hayden, so I rode my horse, Nazimova, down the slope. One hunting season Frank walked me five miles down the trail from Camp Marian, up the mountains where we hunted all day, then back up the trail to camp again where I cooked supper for the hunting party even though it was only tomato soup. I was so tired I didn't even clean my rifle, a cardinal sin. The buck I killed that day, the last day of the hunting season, outweighed the prize-winning buck at Piper and Taft's in Seattle, but we could not get it there in time for the weighing.

Of course among those we packed in were many interesting people. There was the sweet Scotsman, who named the owls Broad-faced Hens and called Mt. Mystery and her companion peak Mt. Misery and Mt. More Misery. He would have me sing Scotch songs in the evening around the campfire, but admitted that his favorite song was not Scotch, but was "Mother Macree." He said he had been in most of the mountain ranges in Europe and that while there might be more outstanding single peaks he felt that as a range the Olympics had them all beat. He did yearn for his native Scotland, however, and I've often wondered if he ever went back.

Then there was the well-known photographer who wanted me to pose nude as an Indian maid on

a rock in the river. Who me? No way!

The person I will never forget was a lawyer from Seattle who was responsible for one of our few tragedies on the trail, and one of my ugliest jobs with the pack train. Hardtack was our most temperamental horse. A big, raw-boned bay, he never really wanted to be a packhorse. He even had been seen cavorting with an elk herd one moon-lit night in Dose Meadows. Once he tried to bull his way under a partly fallen tree on the trail. He happened to be carrying two large boxes of dynamite for the Forest Service at the time.

Back to the lawyer. We met him almost completely exhausted on the trail. Frank, in an unfortunately generous mood offered to put his pack on Hardtack. Hardtack already had a large crosscut saw looped on top of his pack with the wooden handles tied together. When we got to Dose Meadows Ranger Station, the man was eager to get his pack, but was told he would have to wait a few minutes until Frank, or Jerry could get it for him. We were busy with our horses and did not see him disregard orders and try to get his pack. Inadvertently, he loosed one end of the saw which began to whip around violently, al-most taking off his head and that of Jerry who was next to him. Hardtack, terrified, began running and bucking down the trail. With every jump the big saw was cutting into his legs and flanks. We finally caught him and Frank dressed his wounds as best he could. We had commitments and had to continue over the pass and down the Elwha. We were gone several days and the weather was hot. When we finally got back to Dose Meadows, Hardtack had been dead for several days and was in an ad-vanced stage of decomposition. It was impossible to bury the big horse in one piece. Jerry had continued down the Elwha so there was only Frank and me. Frank had a large cut on his hand which

he had received while trying to catch Hardtack,
so the danger of infection was too great for him
to risk doing the job. I was the one who had to
cut up Hardtack. As I said, I could do anything
Frank thought I could.

Oh, yes, about my little bear. I had
stayed at the ranger station to do some cooking
while Frank went up into Lost country. There
he came across a she-bear with three cubs. She
put one of the cubs up a tree and ran off with
the other two. Frank couldn't resist capturing
the third and bringing her down to me. We stayed
in the hills for about two weeks before we came
back home again to Blyn. In that time the cub
had accepted me as her mother. I kept her at
home until the time came for me to go back to
college. If Woodland Park had been as fine as
it is now, I probably would have given her to them,
but finally decided it would be better to take her
into the woods behind the house. There still were
huckleberries on the bushes, the woods were full
of downed logs teeming with ants and our orchard
had windfall apples on the ground. At that time
I had long hair and sometimes wore it in a bun in
back held with hairpins. She used to love to sit
in my lap and pick the pins out of my hair until
it hung down.

That last day I took her into the woods
until I found a downed rotten log. It was full
of ants. I took off her collar and chain and
held her in my lap. By that time she was quite
big and barely fit. She took the hairpins out of
my hair and let it down. I put her onto the log
and left her scooping up ants. My mother said
that she came back several times for apples. She
said that she looked well-kept. Of course I never saw her again. I would never capture a wild
thing again, but I do cherish memories of the
time I had her, and it does give me status with
my grandchildren.

My packing days ended with my graduation
from the university and my marriage. My husband
bought into the pack train and for a couple of
years worked with Frank. However, with no hunters to pack in most of the profit had gone and
the pack train was given up. I loved my days as
a girl packer, but now am quite content just to
admire my mountains from afar.

MARIAN TAYLOR

A Conversation Before Returning to Tehran

(Sausalito, California - October 13, 1983)

"I tell you this because I feel something special
between us. You say you are a writer and I think,
though my English is not so good, I can still tell
you much about my country.

"But, my new friend, please remember you must
not use my name in your work. The spies...you
never know where they walk. I always feel their
eyes on me, even when I sleep. When my daughter
calls me by telephone from here in your country,
I can hear them on the line. They don't even
bother to hide this. They listen as she tells me
about school and her new friends, but what can I
say to her? That I know that where she is, it is
better? I cannot. That would be treason in their
ignorant eyes.

"I hope you never feel how difficult it is to live
with freedom and then have it taken from you as
if it was an old piece of clothing. Only
when I am on the plane will I really be able to
thank God that my two children are safe here in
America. Only then will I be close enough to Him.

"My husband, you see it is very hard for him to
leave his work. They would never allow him to
take his savings out of Iran. We would have to
start from nothing in your country and at our ages,
you see, this is sometimes just too difficult.

"On the plane from London to Tehran, I must change
out of clothes like these and drape my *chador* to
cover my face as if I lived decades ago in time.
But I tell you, if I dressed like this...this
flower in my hair and these stockings on the streets

of my country, they could have me shot. It is
too horrible the things they do.

"It is even more difficult because I can't talk
about this to the women of my family who have
lived in America a long time now. They have
never known our country like I have seen it.
They can only speak of the old days...before the
revolution when Americans were our closest friends.
But now the Americans have all come home and the
people left are too afraid to say what they really believe. If one is educated like our kind,
you know, this revolution is like being reborn
into hell.

"So are you very surprised by my words? You see...
it is never enough to read the newspapers. America
is already bored with news about Iran. We, the
ones like myself, are alone with this war now.
Even the young ones living here from my country
have heard enough.

"I will celebrate tonight, but not from my heart
because tomorrow I must return to live in fear
that the spies will see through these veiled
eyes all the way into these kind of thoughts."

                                    MARY LOU SANELLI

116

Some Background

During the 1960's and early 1970's, the Shah of Iran began to treat the riches of his country as if they were personal property. Court ceremonial in that country was so elaborate that there was continual bowing and pomp; visitors had to leave the royal house by walking backwards. Similar absurdities were numerous. Historically, it has been said that the more rigid the ceremonial in a court, the more likely the people of a country are to suffer under oppression.

Iran was supported by the United States during these years. American oil companies at the end of 1973 still dominated the oil market and the dollar was the currency for international oil transactions. But following the October War of 1973, the Arab countries had for the first time used "the oil weapon" and cut back supplies to the West. Iran did not join them. It was the Shah, the West's most trusted ally in the Middle East, who continued to sell oil to the Western nations.

The most remarkable thing about Iran during the boom years of the 1970's was the total absence of any attempt to involve the people in any form of political representation. The years of the Shah's absolutism were in full swing. Women could receive 75 lashes for accepting a drink. Homosexuals were arbitrarily executed as were thousands of other torture victims. The Shah was known to house vats of acid to dispose of the bodies.

Pressure to conceal the truth about what was happening was very strong. The Shah had totally cut himself off from the reality of how most of his people still lived. He accepted this as the price of progress. The social fabric of the country unraveled. Each section of the community felt that those above them were getting the most. There were some fifty thousand American businessmen and their families living in Iran. They were

the most well paid, fed, and housed in Tehran.
In 1975, two American men were shot in the city.
The revolution of the people began.

Just after the rise of Ayatollah Khomeini
and the Shah's expulsion, Iranian feminists began
to organize to protect what little rights they
had been granted under the Shah. These women, as
a group, were constantly threatened with torture
and death. It is not known how many did die and
still die for such basics as wanting an education,
a job, or wearing Western dress. Anything the
women of Iran did separately from their men was
regarded as being anti-revolutionary. Abortion
was immediately abolished after Khomeini's rise
to power. No one even dared speak of it. The
women fought (and continue to fight) to protect
what few nurseries were still operating. They
continue to fight for equal pay as well, if they
can manage to find someone to employ them outside
of domestic obligations.

Clearly, women suffered oppression under the
Shah, as did all of the common people. But under
the Ayatollah, things became even worse. He con-
doned the Moslems for attacking women demonstrators
and for disrupting any attempt at their organized
rallies. Perhaps one of the most tragic acts put
upon the women of Iran was (and is) the mandatory
wearing of the *chador* (or total body veiling) which
serves as the ultimate symbol for female submission.

MARY LOU SANELLI

118

Das Neue Kleid

Das neue kleid is German and means "the new
dress." Most likely you are thinking, "Why not say
so in the first place and save a lot of time?"
Be charitable and don't think I am showing off.
When I was getting ready to tell this story, I
really did think to say: I'll tell about the
time in 1945 and my new dress; but you see, saying something in German or something in English
makes, to me, all the difference in the world.
It has to do with before and after, with two en-
tirely different times, emotions, loves, loyalties,
and places. I do hope that you see what I mean
when my tale is told.

My grandmother had a little saying, and it
was surprising how often she used it. She lived
to be almost 100 years old. The saying went like
this: "Alle guten Dinge sind drei." I heard the
same in Spain, Austria, and America: Good things
come in threes. But when I got sick, for thing
#1, and she had business problems, for thing #2,
she would announce triumphantly for us to expect
the worst, for "all bad things come in threes"
as well. You see, three has a special quality
about it. It's a mysterious number, packed with
symbolism. I am not surprised, therefore, that
I inherited that special feeling for three; one
has to inherit something from one's grandmother.
Now to my story.

Without thinking about it, not consciously
at least, I have divided my youth during the years
from 1939 to 1945 into three parts; three good
things or three bad things, depending on one's
point of view.

Nineteen forty-five was a terrible, terrible
year in Europe, regardless from whose point of
view. Certainly a fiendish regime and a holocaust
were in their final hours, but the price paid was
high. No bells were rung, most being broken along
with the bell-ringers. However, I am not writing

a war story. The world is filled with these. I
am anxious to tell you a life story. The world
is filled with these, too, but sometimes I think
they are less heard of—and not so popular.

I think it was in March of 1945 when a German
sergeant darted up into the tower, outside Darm-
stadt, where I was conscripted to observe and
report "enemy aircraft activity," and told me to
come along and save my skin: the Americans had
arrived. All the other girls from my barrack had
been put on a bus and were gone. Confusion reigned
and "rules" lost their power. The sergeant was
"in charge" and told me to get behind him on his
motorbike and he would get me caught up with the
rest of the group. This was not to be. The bus
had been destroyed and everyone killed. So began
the strangest trip of my life.

I no longer have the slightest idea how long
I was on that motorbike; it does not really matter.
The next picture in my story is that of a very
typical, ancient farm. Sinister and dark is my
memory of it—a wall enclosing all the buildings,
a heavy gate to stop entrance into the farmyard,
and a farmer to match the scene. I slept in a
barn with others around me, none of whom I had
ever seen before, including a quite pregnant woman with calm, great eyes and a steadiness about
her that felt good. The sergeant was gone. He
had to go. He was a soldier and the enemy was
advancing fast, but there was really nowhere to
go, poor man. Everything that happened next
could easily fill a book, so we'll skip most of
it. It is not that important in my memory.

My next memory of interest is that of everyone crowded into the cellar under the farmhouse,
waiting for the storm to pass. In time, the distant, awful noises changed to a rumble, and the
rumble came closer and closer—then voices: a
tongue not familiar and yet, familiar to me

in a strange way. Our good farmer, engulfed in
terror, propelled me to the airslit and hoisted
me up to look. Jeeps, trucks, and men—the farmyard exploded with white stars—Americans! But
oh, they looked and sounded quite different from
what I had imagined and yet.... Bang, bang, bang!
The heroic farmer swung me around and pushed me
ahead of himself to the steep steps. Here I was,
terrified, staring up into the eyes of a man with
a gun and, yes, a bayonet. We stared at each
other a considerably long time. I had the definite
feeling that he was terrified too, with all of us
huddled in a dark cellar, eyes turned toward him
and the farmer hissing into my ear: "You are educated—talk to him, talk or...." Isn't this silly! I was never told in school what is proper
English in the case of a chance meeting between
a young lady and a man with a gun and bayonet in
a root cellar. So I said: "How do you do?" It
was obviously not the proper thing to say, for
the soldier put his weapon under his arm and grinned
and a conversation such as one gets used to only
under certain circumstances began. He pointed,
and presented a very fine pantomime of a hungry
man. Behind me in a bin were potatoes. Yes, yes
that's it. I held up a potato. "No, no, no, no!"
I held up a beet (meant for fodder). "No, no, no,
no!" Next came a carrot. I grew desperate for
we had *nothing* else. Our visitor did not think
so. He began "crying and sobbing." Of course,
of course. Dorothea, how stupid you are: an
onion! Quickly, I pulled an onion from the
braided strand hanging from the ceiling and, step
by step, cautiously went up, arm outstretched,
offering the onion. He took it, bit into it,
and joyfully exclaimed "Cebolla! Gracias!" and
was gone. My first American spoke Spanish. What
a surprise.
    I told you this lengthy episode because it

was this incident which took the fearfulness out
of me. Americans were people: some did not even
speak English and bit into onions for which they
risked quite a lot. I began to plan. The first
chance came quickly to prove my new theory. The
woman with the big eyes and quiet ways was going
to have her baby. Just before her pains began,
a jeep had driven through the village with an
American shouting through a megaphone, this time
in German, that no one was to get on the street
or highway. We were to stay put. The woman knew
where the midwife lived; she had come to the village with a group of refugees days before. If
her baby was to be born with proper care, she
needed someone to go with her. So I went and we
made it. I believe that nothing is by chance and
often, reminiscing, it seems my life alone is
proof enough for me. On the way back to the
farm, I saw American vehicles approaching and
ducked into a bakery and found—no, not bread,
but "grapevine" news of refugees planning to get
together early in the morning and, as a group,
trying to get back west in the direction of
Frankfurt, Meinz, Wiesbaden, and so forth. Meeting place: this very bakery. It was taking a
big chance, but what else was there to do? I
would take the chance.

I got to the bakery in the early morning on
the appointed day, but I found no one. Yes, one
lady. We waited, but no one else arrived and, as
it was becoming light, we had to get out. I have
not the foggiest memory of how we figured out the
route, or who advised us. We simply took a bearing
and aimed ourselves in the general direction: west.
All seemed to go well for several hours. We became confident, walking closer to the highway.
Approaching very fast from behind us came some
vehicles and down we went. They never saw us.
Or did they? Well, Americans not only bit into

onions and spoke Spanish, they also were the
fastest "backer-uppers" I ever saw. The last jeep
from the convoy backed up and someone jumped out
and cleared the ditch all in one. My companion
stared, rose, met him, and shook hands. I am
sure I need not dwell on my astonishment. The
American was a doctor, and so was my lady-companion.
She had helped him a few days before in an incident involving civilians. He had seen us and
recognized her. He sternly admonished us, point-
ing out our unlawful travelling. Back he went
into the jeep and off he went, we thought forever.
Not so. Again he returned, exceeding his former
backing-up speed, tossed us two packages and even
more sternly told us that which was for me a con-
stant truth: "You're hungry, I know!" I looked
at the olive-brown parcel. How does it open?
What does it hold? Off went the jeep down the
empty road, at breakneck speed, leaving me in ut-
ter puzzlement, but not for long. The doctor
had an absolute passion for backing up. Faster
than ever he came. I just knew he was sorry to
have parted from the parcel and would want it
back. To this day I can feel the anguish. Out
he jumped, out came a knife, and the packages were
opened—lesson in the use of tiny, funny can
openers. The doctor dug his heel into the ground,
swirled around a few times, put something white
into the small hollow he had made, lit it and put
an opened can on it commanding: "Eat it when warm."
With one leap, he was again in the jeep and off.
It all took a minute; at least it seems to me so
to this day. I expected him back, backing up.
But no, I never saw him again. May he always be
blessed. Well, Americans bite into onions, speak
English and Spanish, have a passion for backing
up, jumping in and out of jeeps, and are fast and
efficient. So far, so good! Here, however, my
fortune came to an abrupt end, at least for a while.

My companion was strange from the beginning.
She was alternately chatty and friendly and, as
suddenly, totally silent, withdrawn and hostile.
We saw no one: a few convoys went by in both
directions, some with red crosses, but no one
else. It was terribly depressing. Neither of us
had anything, we were uncertain of our whereabouts,
uncertain of the territory, and uncertain of the
war situation. We had only in common the desire
to get away from where we were and go west. Soon
she ceased speaking altogether. How long we stayed
together I don't know. I became terribly fright-
ened of her. When she insisted, again and again,
on roads I felt were wrong, we parted like two
sleepwalkers, heedless of all dangers, each in
her chosen direction. I was on this, my strangest
of all journeys, alone.

I had tied a white handkerchief, my sole
luxury, around my arm, naively imagining it a
sign of peace and neutrality. The white handkerchief gave me confidence—it was my shield
and symbol. I can't tell you why I needed to go
through a dense forest, but it must have figured
into the plans formulated at the bakery long ago.
The forest floor was so clear of brush it felt
swept. Beautiful trees towered above. Many
forests in Germany are thus. As I went between
the trees, I heard shots. It may sound unbeliev-
able to you, but though I heard the whining of
whatever missiles, it never occurred to me that
they may have been directed at me, so strongly
did I believe in the power of my white handkerchief and my clear conscience. So I continued
to walk.

Coming, in time, across a field with helmets
strewn about, German helmets and those to whom
once the helmets gave protection, I was not even
moved. Man is a strange creation! Our emotions

and reactions, our best and lowest instincts,
seem so tied up with our stomachs and our physical
condition! Here I came across a place of blood
and brutal death and simply stumbled on, as if I
did not care.

A few hours later I was almost defeated by
the loss of my white handkerchief. I had come
to a stream and, bending over, used it to wash
my face. It fell in and floated off. The white
cloth disappearing down the stream, floating away,
leaving me without my symbol of peace: it was
misery, total disaster and a crucial point. Who
cared for a girl who was lost between two armies—
or was it three or twenty? What did it matter
anyway? What is a life or two—or three or twenty
or thousands or tens of thousands? I felt more
alone than ever before or since.

In my surrender, I became part of my sur-
roundings and, in my abandonment, felt a response
of strength. I heard birds and knew it was summer.
The stream had taken my handkerchief away, but not
out of mischief or viciousness. The stream had
to take it once it rested on the wavelets and
rivulets. The men who killed one another were
not vicious or hateful—surely, many of them may
have been tender lovers, husbands, fathers, friends,
students filled with curiosity and plans. They,
too, had been dropped into a stream and carried
off. Healing, mending tears washed away that
which had almost become an insulation inside myself. I could not sit here: I had life and an
obligation to find out what life was about.

I got up and, within a few minutes, knew
myself to be on a bluff overlooking a highway
winding and winding away, off into the distance.
Toy vehicles appeared on it. No, not toys—war
machines—coming and going. It is at this point
in my story that I am glad not to be giving a
report on historic events, though often enough I

have been told to do so, for I neither remember
the exact spot where I stood nor the dates. Below
me, history was made without my knowledge. I observed, ignorant of the occasion, man's surrender
to events. Americans driving, could it be, toward
me and toward the Soviet red stars. Red stars!
That was the one thing I wanted to avoid. I turned
and left, forgetting my exhaustion until not even
the thought of red stars could keep my legs moving.

A big archway tower marked a village, which
must have been in another world, it was so quiet
and sleepy. White fences and gates guarded houses
which belonged to history, were loved and had faces
like people. The people in them, however, did not
want me. They feared just another refugee or D.P.,
and a dirty one at that! The end of the tiny town,
to my memory, seemed to spread into a broad, sunny
valley. A gate was open and, not only that, Love
in person stood at the door. The rest is a dream.
Only once in life do things of this nature happen,
and that's for the best I suppose. The old man,
beautiful and stern, came to the gate along a
little path which had an intricate pattern of dark
red and pink bricks. He put his arm around me,
leading me into a big kitchen. Never since did I
see so much gentleness and graciousness. He first
took a tin basin and poured water from the "reser-
voir" on the end of the woodstove. Next, he went
for a towel. He tested the water with his elbow,
like a young mother would the bath for her infant.
The old man knelt down and undid my boots, peeling
gently what was left of the socks off my feet. He
was The Healer. I kept rummaging in my mind for
whom he reminded me of. At that time I did not
know for sure—today I do. He did not say much,
but he went to a corner cabinet with white porcelain
knobs and took out a pot and bandages. When all
was over, he fed me something warm, simply picked
me up, carried me into another room, put me on a

huge featherbed and left. When I awoke, I did not
know whether I had slept a day or a year. I was
clean and had on a huge, very scratchy nightgown.
The old man had seven daughters; all lived with
him and several had lost their husbands. The old
man had to give up his only son, the son who was
to inherit the farm and carry on his name.

He told me that I had not gone west as I
had hoped. Much later I discovered that I may
have observed an event connected with the linking-
up of American and Russian troops. At that time,
all I knew was the experience of my first rest in
years. I felt safe, but I also knew I had to go
west and try to pick up my life by bits and pieces.
First, however, we must speak of my fairy godmother,
the young counterpart of the old man.

The friend of the family was a terribly de-
formed hunchback girl with the most twinkling,
mischievous eyes, the sweetest face and the clev-
erest hands you ever saw. She lived next to the
tower and had a room with a sewing machine. Her
business was that of the local dressmaker, as well
as repair and remodeling expert. She was proud
of that distinction.

All seven daughters of Herr Moor were considerably larger than myself and it presented some
problems. The dear remodeling expert did her best,
but we could not come up with a dress that I could
wear on the next leg of my journey. We had years
of rationing behind us—not much left to share.
Hannelle, the dressmaker, had an inspiration.
From a secret hiding place, she retrieved a huge
"swastika" flag. You heard right!! Oh, she had
no patriotic sentiments, but she could not bear
to have this much good cotton go to waste; so she
hid the big flag that had fluttered once from the
tower next to her room. She made us sit around
the big flag and carefully take the stitches out
to retrieve the black of the emblem and the white

of the circle. We had to wash the parts and press
them and she made my new dress. Hannelle created
das neue kleid. It was very, very red and I
wondered secretly how one could hide in a dress
like that. It had a white Peter Pan collar, white
cuffs, and black trim. Believe me, it was the
most glorious and the most awful dress I have
ever worn, but it was a gift of selfless love and
it was magic! Really magic!!

When I left, I carried a small sack with me
and I blazed like a flame as I walked toward
Frankfurt. I could not bear looking down on my
new dress, so I simply looked ahead. For nine
days—three times three—I walked alone, wrapped
securely in the magic of the old man, his daughters,
and Hannelle's *neues kleid*. Then I fell in with
a group of refugees and, after that, with a mother
and daughter. They considered my dress with grave
looks, but after I offered to take turns pulling
their wagon to Frankfurt, they relented. When we
got to the city, the mother invited me to share
her own home for a rest.

My red dress blazed through Wiesbaden and its
magic brought me to a job as an interpreter with
the Americans. It was the cause for mirth and
many strange looks but, for me, it was a symbol
of a new era, a new life. A new dress—not for
me alone I was hoping. Something good was made
out of something hateful. It had to be ripped
apart, cleaned, and recreated into a useful garment!
Surely you can see why I had to call my story
"Das Neue Kleid." Calling it "The New Dress"
would not do.

DOROTHEA AMMANN PARES MORGAN

Making Room for the Light

for Ru

I run the rock-flung tide line
to McCurdy Point, a newly-contoured
beach emerging like a phoenix
from last night's storm. You have given
me a named destination, McCurdy Point,
an insignificant spit of sand and rock
beneath a crumbling bluff, today
surrounded by long, slow, curling
breakers like the open Pacific.
I have run this territory before
but now I have a name
for where I'm headed: McCurdy Point.
This rhymes with Purdy, the women's
prison in this state. I lift
my feet up and put them down, chanting:
McCurdy, Purdy, McCurdy, Purdy.

The sand gives way beneath my feet
and my heels dig deep. The beach
is littered with dead and dying
chitons, pink, fleshy vaginas
gaping at me. Running to McCurdy Point
I wonder: are these Straits
the final graveyard for all
the vaginas ripped from women,
a sacred burial ground for the refuse
of hysterectomy after criminal hysterectomy,
at rest, here, near the dark ocean,
come to the safety of salt water at last?

I am still on my way, running
to McCurdy Point, thinking of you,
me, the other women I know and don't
know, the ones I have a hard time seeing
because they are in prison
as I am in prison, though I am running
west on this exposed tideland
and free to do so. I recall
how you tell me you walked
this same beach a few days ago,

129

minutes after I did. I watched
you smile and remember how it was,
this first solitary walk in - in—
and then you hesitate, all conversation
halts while some part of you whirrs
like a movie camera focused
on an internal calendar, pages flipping
through days and months just like
in the old movies—your first solitary walk
in a year.

The Straits breathe long and deep,
water rising and falling
like a giant slumbering breast.
I am on my way, closer to McCurdy Point
and I know this for certain:
we are eager jailers
for the jailed self.
I am walking in the blue and gold
dwindling day, my body reaching for
the light, another self groping
in the dark where I find you
silhouetted in the dim grey cell,
your two sons beside you.
I am walking to McCurdy Point,
gazing through a single barred window,
searching for the first hesitant star
and I must tell you again that I am,
you are, we are, *in prison.* I repeat
this fact because our minds
are dulled by routine, the harsh
grate of keys in locks and I know
we could sleep a lifetime,
our faces turned
to the wall.

It is not enough to say:
'we make our own prisons,'
but saying 'prison' is a beginning.

There are bricks and mortar,
roof joists and solid beams
others bring to the construction site
and they take pleasure doing so,
I would be lying if I did not say this.
These others are: law and custom,
court and welfare worker. They are
judge and jury, and in this state,
executioner. They are faceless
members of corporate boards,
computer conglomerates, munitions
makers, stockholders, congressmen,
senators. Yes, they are professors,
psychiatrists and single-minded gynecologists,
eager surgeons and ministers professing
belief in a loving god. They are well-meaning
fathers, dutiful husbands, sensuous lovers
and innocent sons, though you struggle
to find ways this will not be so.

I am almost to the spit of sand
when I think of another friend
who shows me a window in a room
lined with books, a room in her house
where light pours through
a once-solid wall. When I say,
look how much light, she nods.
What is unsaid, what we are unsure of:
is there enough light
for us to claim each other
in the dark cells, enough light
to arrive, sweaty and breathless
at McCurdy Point; ample
and abundant light for the unknown
and forgotten, the myriad jailed selves
inside Purdy, waiting for our prayers
to free them?

The sun is down and done early,
swallowed by the same clouds
that hide the mountains. I climb
onto a storm-tossed snag, slippery
and gnarled with labyrinthine roots.
I can see the line of trees
on Protection Island and imagine
seals sleeping, gulls hovering
above them. In the last solar glow,
kelp floats off McCurdy Point, gleaming
stars fallen to earth and reluctant
to abandon light. I look out
to the darkening Straits and there
you are, hoisting sail, catching
a fresh wind out of the west,
your two small sons with you, everyone
leaning with the boat into the wind.
I shout across the water:
we are making room for the light,
we are making room.

CHRISTINA V. PACOSZ

Seam-Itza

Essentially this is a true story. My stepfather,
Frank Vincent, told it to me years ago. I was too
young to press for details, therefore I am not
sure whether it was Frank's mother or grandmother
to whom it happened. If it was his mother, it
happened somewhere near Graysmarsh Farm. If it
was his grandmother, it happened in Port Townsend.

She had left no note.... The little house
glowed. The floors had been scrubbed, the windows
sparkled and on the board table, covered with her
favorite blue-checked tablecloth, her precious
blue willow-ware pitcher held a few late blooming
wild flowers. On the counter by the kitchen pump
were two freshly baked blackberry pies. Their
aroma almost hid the faint, foreign odor of the
room. Piles of freshly laundered clothes were
stacked neatly on the bed near mounds of newly
darned socks. Hanging at the windows were crisp,
newly laundered curtains, hanging from the
door————!

*****

Alexander Vincent had come to Port Townsend
as a boy. He was tall; a distinguished looking
man whose grandparents had fled from France
during the French Revolution. Although not titled,
they were aristocrats and in grave danger of
death. The family fled first to England and then
to America, making their home in New York State.
There, the family put down permanent roots, but
there was a spirit of adventure in the second
generation and Alexander joined other adventurous
people and went west.

Seam-Itza also was an aristocrat. Daughter
of the chief of the Port Townsend Clallams, she
was proud of her heritage. Many strings of
dentalium adorned her throat and head. Her hair
was as black as Kah-kah's wing, her eye as bright
as Chil-chil, the star. She carried her head

proudly as became a chief's daughter. Her tiny feet and shapely legs, showing as she stepped forth in her cattail skirts, had caught the eye of many a young brave. Although of marriageable age, Seam-Itza had not as yet given her heart. Her father, in no hurry to have his daughter leave the family house, had, at her urging, refused many offers of marriage.

The stories do not tell exactly how Alexander met the lovely Seam-Itza, but he must have been deeply in love because he and Seam-Itza were married, not only in the tribal tradition, but also in the white man's way. Seam-Itza legally became Alexander's wife. For some time the young couple continued to live in Port Townsend but finally moved to the Sequim area and settled down on part of what is now Graysmarsh Farm. Here several children, including Frank, were born.

Alexander had written many letters home describing the beauty of his bride. One thing he had neglected to do, probably because it seemed unimportant to him. He had not told his family that he had married an Indian girl.

One day a sailing vessel dropped anchor off Port Williams. A beautifully gowned, handsome woman disembarked. After making inquiries, a team was hired and the journey to the Vincent home was made. Arriving at the little home, the woman asked the driver to wait lest there be some mistake. Seam-Itza, looking out the window, saw the beautiful white lady approaching the house. She gave a quick pat to her hair, a twist to her dress, and was ready to open the door at the stranger's knock.

The stranger smiled graciously at the little Indian woman and said, "Please tell your mistress, Mrs. Vincent, that Alexander's sister, her sister-law, is here to pay a visit."

Seam-Itza was delighted. Excitedly she said,

"Come in, come in. I am Alexander's wife. I am Mrs. Vincent."

Without a word the beautiful lady turned away, got into the wagon, and ordered the driver to leave.

Seam-Itza walked a few feet into the yard and watched the disappearing wagon. She turned and walked slowly, sadly but determinedly into the house.

No one actually was witness to the events that followed. They were pieced together later. It was not Alexander who was the first to enter the little cabin. One of the sons came home from work and it was he who saw the result of his aunt's visit. He found no note. Seam-Itza could not write. He saw the pies and stacks of laundry. He saw the crisp curtains hanging at the window, and hanging from the door was Seam-Itza.

MARIAN TAYLOR

An Anthropologist's View

The beautifully written and powerful story
of the Clallam woman, Seam-Itza, illustrates the
clash between two different political systems
and its devastating effect on human lives. Super-
ficially, the political structure of the European
aristocracy and that of the Pacific Coast Indians
of North America was similar. Both were ruled by
powerful men whose positions were inherited, along
with their wealth, power, and prestige. In both
societies greater and lesser nobility existed;
some of whom were quite wealthy and powerful.
The power and privilege enjoyed by members of noble families depended, in part, on currying favor
with their powerful ruling relatives, and in part
on social, economic and political shrewdness (and
of course, luck). In both cultures nobility made
the most advantageous marriages possible—to other
members of noble families—in order to increase
(or gain access to) power, wealth, and prestige.
In both systems advantageous marriages were arranged, often without consent of the bride and
groom.
But there was a crucial difference between
the European aristocracy and the Clallam. European power, prestige, wealth, and birthright
were passed patrilineally, through the father to
his sons only. Women did not inherit wealth or
power, unless there was no legitimate male heir.
Women, then, were noble only insofar as they were
related to noble men. They could not own or pass
on their status, and a man might marry a noble
woman in order to gain access to her father's
wealth and power, never hers.
This was not, however, true for Pacific
Coastal tribes. In general, they were ambilineal,
which means wealth, power, and prestige were
passed either through the male or the female line.
Women could, and did, inherit songs, dances, cop-
pers, titles, power, and prestige from their
fathers or their mothers, and these they possessed

137

in their own right, so they could pass them on
to their heirs. A noble man, then, would marry
the daughter of a chief because she, herself,
owned the rights to songs and dances (symbols of
great prestige) and could pass them to her children. Intertribal marriages were arranged in order to have tribal access thereafter to a particular song or dance. So great was the prestige of
these women that, in many tribes, a woman might
be married many times, so that more men might have
access to her wealth. Rather than the dowry a
woman in Europe was required to bring to her husband's family (a symbol of the woman's economic
liability), a Clallam woman's family received
great gifts (bride price) from the groom's family,
as she was considered an economic asset.

Just why Seam-Itza would choose to marry a
white man is a mystery. Undoubtedly her father
could have demanded a substantial bride price
from an Indian suitor. Perhaps Alexander's
aristocratic background influenced her father.
Perhaps he understood that the white men were gain-
ing power in the region, and he wanted to make an
alliance. Love would not have been a particularly
important factor, although it might have made
Seam-Itza put pressure on her father to allow the
marriage. At any rate, Seam-Itza would have considered herself, as the daughter of a chief, as
good as (or better than) her husband's sister.
His sister, however, even had she known of her
sister-in-law's nobility, would never have considered Seam-Itza her equal. Not only did she come
from a culture in which women did not have power
in their own right, but she came from a culture
which was extremely ethnocentric and regarded
all non-Europeans as inferior, primitive, and
worthless. It must have been inconceivable to
her that her aristocratic brother had married a
"savage."

The snub Seam-Itza received from her sister-in-law would not have been so terrible had she been a commoner—or, indeed, a slave. But Seam-Itza was used to respect. I do not know if suicide to protest a terrible injustice was common among Clallams, but I do know it was frequent among other American Indians. When someone had been done a dreadful wrong, the only way one could reclaim one's dignity and at the same time heap scorn upon and publicly shame the wrongdoer was to commit suicide. It was approved of as the ultimate act of dignity and courage, and at the same time the most terrible insult to the perpetrator of the original slight. In most Pacific Coastal groups it was certainly not considered immoral.

Seam-Itza chose death with dignity to shame her sister-in-law and to assert her right to power and respect. This act, viewed from our perspective as tragic but from hers as the ultimate act of strength and defiance, illustrates the human consequences of the battle between two different cultures in which power and prestige are understood in different terms. If we are able to step outside our culture and set aside our ethnocentrism for a moment, we see in Seam-Itza's suicide the ultimate act of power, dignity, strength, and courage—a triumph instead of a tragedy.

JOYCE MORDEN

Gate of Horn

Opening my garden gate opens me onto sacred
space. Here I leave the distracted world and
enter a place of personal power...a quiet, ordered
world which has over the years grown into a sea-
sonal shrine to Gaia, the Great Mother, our Mother
Earth. The garden is fenced and densely planted,
enclosed and protected from intrusion or interruption. The view to the south is past my farm
to the foothills of the Olympics; to the north
lies the Strait and Vancouver Island. The water
through the trees gives me deep satisfaction....

I laid the garden out as a mandala, with
paths to the four directions radiating from a
center point...opening out through circles and
squares. A wicca circle of eight seats defines
an inner round, the center of which is a sundial
and a raised bed of iris. All the raised beds
are built of great cedar boxes; I laid them out
in the figure and parts of a woman...still es-
tablishing the circles and squares of a mandala.
Though not readily apparent to others, the woman who is myself crouches there, growing and
changing her colors through the seasons.

Her head, a carp and lotus pond, points
north; it is grown in with forget-me-nots and
lilies, framed with rhododendron and vine maple.
Beach rocks and shells encircle her throat. The
wide beds of her shoulders carry vegetables and
flowers, her arms point south...growing most of
the family food. Two mounded beds raise up
into breasts richly covered with flowers. At
her navel, her solar plexus, sit the sundial and
iris...ringed with round rocks and fossils,
perennials and moss. Her genital center makes
up my herb garden, for healing and refreshment...
mounded strong and sweet, the cooking herbs, the
drinking herbs, the flowers and leaves of spices.
Her legs and feet get lost in green growths of
mint; the boxes of her feet hold the garden

greens and bulbs, cut flowers and squash.

And, there, between her rounded legs...I
bleed. A sacred spot amidst the growth and
dying back, a place I've set aside where I alone
can go. I return my blood to the earth, to the
life force from which we come...my blood falling
softly, marking a spot not casually visited...
marking the place of my own immutable power. I
squat there, primordial, in quiet watchfulness...
the one time each month that I temporarily turn
my back on farmhouse and family, turn my face to
the wind, to the cold inspiration of the north...
stop the world and reclaim that wilder side of
woman's nature. I review the events of the last
month of living...looking back, looking forward,
in view of the moon's lunar cycle. My emotions,
my mind, my physical body...all these energies
wax and wane through the month. I have learned
to watch them, work with them, respect the rising
and falling. Ideas begin in darkness and grow
into planning. They fill and take form...create
and fall back; fulfilled and done, they decline
and fall away to rest. The lessons of my life
lie close to the heart of the tides...I keep a
rhythm of my own, small tides tied to the moon.

My garden, my allegory, shrine to women's
wisdom through the ages...It is—of course—a
place of rapid growth...and it is, as well, a
source of replacement... of replenishment. It
is a place to return to, a place of storing and
gathering more than just food plants and flowers.
I gather up to myself lost aspects of my psyche,
gather up a wholeness...from which to go on
creating....

II.

   Gardens know two worlds: that foliate world
of the life-giving sun...and the ground itself,
subject to the pull of the moon. The ground....
and the ground underneath, the inner ground of
the psyche, that Underworld of our dreams, visions
and urgings...the subconscious.
   Sometimes as I squat, barefooted...fingers
furrowing the Spring dirt into long lines for
my seeds...I find myself staring down a deep
hole, one of those gates to the Underworld.
A mountain beaver, gopher or mole hole...deep
and round and dark...there, under the edge of
the herbs or a bush, deep and terrible...the
darkness drops away, into the ground. And there,
down around the first corner, down and behind the
first turn....stands Hecate, our dark side, guard-
ing the Underworld. Exiled and misunderstood,
excommunicated and suppressed...closer to each
woman than she is to herself...Hecate stands
silent vigil within us. Those holes in the ground
I never stop up or fill in...they are somehow like
the gates to the inner ground of our being.
Hecate stands there, dark and necessary..old as
stone, cold and cthonic. I honor her with my
blood and my fear. She is within and I need to
know how to reach her. I leave her holes alone,
leave soft words of love and the sweet herbs of
summer. She gives me insight, knowledge and
wholeness; she is Dark Demeter, Black Isis,

who watches life's seasons...whose mystery is our

Oneness, whose gift is rebirth out of darkness.

SUSAN OLIVER

144

Contributors' Notes

Diane Allen is a partner in A & A Arts. She has been doing commercial and fine art in Port Townsend for the last twelve years. Many of her cartoons are still in print. She is an active member of a Womanspirit group in Port Townsend.

Arie Anderson resides at the Port Angeles Convalescent Home and according to Janie Roberts, "has accomplished more in her life time than most people." Her family came across the continent in covered wagons. She married Rowland Anderson, a lifelong mate up until 1970. She was a school teacher in Oregon. Arie is 92.

Carol Jane Bangs has a Ph.D in English Literature from the University of Oregon and has two books of poetry to her credit, most recently, **The Bones of the Earth**, New Directions, 1983. She is currently director of literature programs at Centrum.

Aryana Bates is a Junior at Crescent High School, Joyce Washington. She was president of her Sophmore class and is a member of National Honor Society and recently received National honors for an essay contest. She also spent two weeks in Olympia as a Senate Page.

Robin Biffle "I am mostly occupied with the little business at my typewriter and the tasks which sustain a family and home. I strive for a certain perfection. I try not to be distracted from the possibilities. I try not to forget."

Maggie Crumley is a native Montanan with reluctant gypsy blood. She has published both poetry and prose.

Alice Derry earned an M.F.A. from Goddard College in 1981. She teaches English at Peninsula College. Her poems have appeared in **Poetry**, **Prairie Schooner**, **Tendril**, **Southern Poetry Review**, and others.

Sharon Doubiago "I was born and raised in Southern California. I began taking college classes at the age of 17 when I was married and pregnant with my first child. The first poem I ever read was H.D.'s **Helen In Egypt**. My only childhood reading had been the Bible and the L.A. Times, both of which I consumed passionately. The child was a boy.
These 8 sources, my parents, my teenage husband, my child, H.D., the discovery that was college, the land and place that is Southern California, the Bible and the L.A. Times are undoubtedly the source of my aesthetics (including the propensity for the "long poem.") I subsequently had a daughter, left the husband, received an M.A. in English literature from Cal State University at Los Angeles in 1969. I have spent my life trying to see the culture into which my children must grow. To prepare them; to prepare myself. My books are **Hard Country**, an epic poem, and **The Book of Seeing With One's Own Eyes** (short stories), to be published by Charles Scribners' Sons 1985. I have lived in Port Townsend, when not on the road, since 1980 when my children left home."

Penelope Gonzales "I was born in Idaho in 1950. My family settled permanently in Washington state in 1963. I graduated from a local high school, and received my B.A. in English and Drama from Whitworth College in 1972. I moved to the Port Townsend area to begin teaching at Chimacum in 1975, and have been teaching for eight years while raising a family of three children. I am currently completing a masters degree in reading through Western Washington University while keeping up with my job, my family, and my writing."

Leslie Hayertz has a B.A. ed. in Spanish and minors in English and Asian Studies. She has traveled and studied extensively in Central and South America. Currently she is director of The Language Center, offering classes in foreign languages, the only business of its kind on the Peninsula. A native of Washington, she has lived in Port Townsend for four years. *Clytemnestra Resolved* is her first published story.

Rachel Herr was born in Chicago, Illinois, but spent most of her childhood in Cleveland, Ohio. Since graduation from Northwestern University in Evanston, Illinois where she was awarded the Edwin L. Shulman Award for Fiction, she has made the Pacific Northwest her home. Her work has been published in the **Seattle Post Intelligencer** and **The Kah Tai Anthology**. She is currently at work completing a collection of short stories. *Leaving Mexico City,* her contribution to this Dalmo'ma, was written during a recent six month tour of Mexico.

Phyllis Hopeck has a B.S. in Fine Arts and Art Education at New York State University, 1972. She currently has an art glass business specializing in custom etched glass design. For the past 12 years she has been involved as a graphic artist in free-lance illustration and design projects, most recently for Copper Canyon and Graywolf Press.

Melanie Humfleet's poems have appeared in **Concerning Poetry, Oyez Review, Dog River Review, The Windless Orchard** and elsewhere. A first collection, **Rattlesnake Corner**, is available through Printery Farm, 153 Benson Road, Port Angeles. A second collection was at press at the time of this submission. Ms. Humfleet lives with her husband, Dennis, in a log cabin they built on the Olympic Peninsula.

Ru Kirk is reportedly alive and well and moulting in Port Townsend. We all await her latest incarnation. She has two sons and has been a single mother more often than not.

Evelyn Livingston worked in publishing in California before moving to Port Townsend. She has completed a novel which took second place at the Pacific Northwest Writers Conference and is currently at work on a collection of short stories.

Dierdrei L. Keegan is 26 years old. She was born in San Rafael, California, and she has been a resident of Port Townsend for approximately four years. Dierdrei is married and has one child. She has an Associate of Arts degree and has taken stone lithography workshops with JoAnn Alber. She has also apprenticed on the restoration of Pogany murals in California. Observation, experimentation, and experience have been her main teachers. Her work has appeared in newspapers and exhibits on the Olympic Peninsula.

Jule Klotter After teaching eighth grade English in Ohio for two years, she journeyed to Southern California to learn how to write. Three years later, she earned a master of Professional Writing degree with emphasis on screenwriting from the University of Southern California. In 1982, she moved to the Peninsula and took a part-time teaching job at Olympic College. Her writing continues. She recently applied to the Writers Guild of America for a screenwriting fellowship.

Frances McEvers was born in Browning, Montana in 1941. She is part Cherokee, a member of the Eastern Band in North Carolina. She attended schools in Seattle, Washington and graduated from Roosevelt High School. She has had short stories published in the Spring and Fall Anthologies of the Port Townsend **Leader**. She has four grown children and currently lives in Chimacum with her husband, Gary.

Phyllis Muse Miller Born on a kitchen table in her parents' tiny Chicago basement apartment to the tune of *Come Josephine in my Flying Machine*, Phyllis Muse fast came to the realization that a good way to get out of that basement was to pretend; imaginary playmates, wealth, successes at schools, and in various neighborhoods. Creating stories for brother, sister, and neighborhood children was "pretending" put on paper. Early high school and college classes in journalism, creative writing, and printing proved beneficial in finding jobs with small-town newspapers and a radio station, and later for a California city.
Phyllis and her husband, Vern Miller, met and dated during their summer employment at the Chicago Zoological Park. Forty-two years and four children later they moved to their hillside home overlooking Sequim and the Straits.
Recent published works include business-oriented articles for a California city newsletter and light poetry and prose for Olympic Peninsula newspapers.
Time permitting, Phyllis enjoys gardening, reading, all forms of the arts, sculpture, dancing, and scanning land and sea from the Miller hillside, but not necessarily in that order.

Joyce Morden has an M.A. in Anthropology from San Francisco State University and is currently on the staff at Peninsula College as an Assistant Professor in Cultural and Physical Anthropology. She spent this last summer at school in Europe.

Dorothea Ammann Pares Morgan was born in Barcelona, Spain. She came in 1947 to the U.S.A. and had her first solo show the following year in Massachusetts.
Dorothea received a thorough and broad education in several fields of the Arts in Europe, the U.S.A. and in Mexico. She holds degrees in Interdisciplinary Education, as well as a B.F.A. and M.F.A.
Dorothea, a painter and printmaker, has most recently studied, painted, drawn, shown, lectured and taught in Alaska, Port Angeles, Washington, Sequim Arts, and Northwest Print Council. Her work has gone to many parts of the world and she has received important awards and won several purchase awards. The artist is residing on a farm near Port Angeles, Washington.

Rusty North has an M.A. in Psychology from Antioch West, 1982. She is a senior citizen, identifies herself as disabled, has produced numerous books, and is very familiar with all aspects of printing. She is currently doing video documentaries of women poets on the Peninsula.

Sharon M. O'Hara was born Sharon Marie Blomlie in Bremerton, Washington. She was trained as a cosmetologist in 1960, first working in California, then Washington. She owned and operated a Salon/Gift Boutique for sixteen years until selling it in 1981. Sharon also bred, raised, showed and sold Quarter Horses during that time. Now retired, but still owning horses, she is an active traveler with and without a horse. She is involved with the Backcountry Horsemen of Washington, Jefferson Search and Rescue, and summers with the Forest Service in Eastern Washington, with a horse.

Susan Oliver Originally from Maine, Susan has traveled extensively throughout the U.S., Canada, Europe, Morocco, and Baja California. She is currently a writer, dancer, mother, marine biologist/botanist living on a farm in Joyce, Washington with her husband and two sons. Using years of research, writing, and dance, she expresses her deep-rooted interests in the ancient worlds of myth and religion in a variety of mediums; most successfully, theatrical dance production for women's gatherings. She has co-edited this publication.

Christina V. Pacosz Born of working class parents in 1946 in Detroit, Michigan, she was raised in a loving atmosphere steeped in Polish Catholicism and radical beliefs. She received a Bachelor of Science degree from Wayne State University in 1970 and taught in public schools in Michigan and Oregon for seven years.
She moved to the Olympic Peninsula and lived a simple life in the woods without electricity or water for almost two years. She emerged in the world again as a poet-in-residence for Portland, Oregon's Metropolitan Arts Commission, conducting residencies at two sites, Children's Museum and Villa St. Rose, a locked institution for girls considered beyond parental control. Upon completion of her residencies, she was selected as book bus driver/coordinator for Plains Distribution, a non-profit organization promoting small press concepts and one of three book buses in operation at the time. She traveled from Fargo, North Dakota to five mid-western states, stopping in dozens of small towns on a pre-arranged itinerary, stumping close to two hundred literary selections culled from a thirteen state region.
She later sought non-arts related jobs, eventually returning to the Peninsula and apprenticing herself to a carpenter. She became involved in social work and advocacy for the low income through a Community Action agency and returned to the arts world. She was selected as a poet-in-the-schools by the Washington State Arts Commission, presenting workshops to nearly 3,000 students based on a dream/myth approach.
Christina's publishing history begins in 1970 and public reading commenced in 1975. She has two books of poems, **Shimmy Up To This Fine Mud**, Poets Warehouse, 1976 (in an edition of 500) and **Notes From the Red Zone**, Seal Press, 1983 (also in an edition of 500).
She regards herself as a professional poet, with an emphasis on "profess." She feels a responsibility to unravel her vision and share her revelation.
Christina was the originator and principal editor of this anthology.

Molly Pearson was born in Columbus, Ohio where she misspent her youth. After graduating from Ohio State University, she taught at Antioch High School, where the administration thought science fiction and filmmaking were real subjects. She is a determined wanderer, having roamed through the U.S., Europe and Central America. She wandered to Port Townsend 10 years ago and was thrilled to discover she couldn't find a job in her chosen field. She has worked as a community outreach worker, commercial sprout grower and correspondent for the Jimmy-Come-Lately Gazette.
She currently digs roots in Irondale, Washington. She is happily married to a hunter-gatherer. They have two children, Lily and Nicholas.

Georgia Richard is a painter, born in Seattle in 1930. In 1942 she moved to California where she studied at Chouinard Fine Arts Institute and worked in architectural mosaics. In 1972 she "came home" to the Northwest and completed a B.A. in aesthetics theory at Evergreen. She has taught and exhibited visual arts, and published short fiction, art reviews, and poetry in Port Townsend.

Janie Roberts has published a book of religious poems about the Olympic Northwest called **This Too Will Pass**. She is a staff writer for the Peninsula College newspaper. She intends to become a biographer.

Mary Lou Sanelli's home port is in Port Townsend, Washington when she is not engaged in commercial fishing operations that take her to southeastern Alaska. She was born in Connecticut and educated at Garland's College for Women in Boston. She has lived in Vermont, Switzerland, France and Mexico as well. Her work has been published in a number of anthologies and magazines including **Poetry Seattle**, **Alaska Magazine**, **Cruising World**, and **The Co-Evolution Quarterly**. Her own collection of poetry was published in 1981 entitled, **A Wandering Portrait**. Recently her work was aired on National Public Radio's **All Things Considered** program, as well as public radio in Alaska.

147

Leslie Oliver Siemer was born in Salt Lake City, Utah, but spent most of her childhood in Colorado in a small town near the New Mexico broder. She attended Colorado State University, where she was awarded a poetry scholarship in 1976. In 1978 she and her husband, Dennis moved to Washington. She has worked as a waitress, trim sawyer, bevel sawyer, ridge nailer and packer in the cedar mills on the Peninsula. At present she is a part time clerk in a small grocery store and a volunteer counselor at the Port Angeles Family Planning Clinic. She has a four year old son, Ian and gardens, cans, grows and dries herbs. She has been interested in writing since the age of seven and takes direction from a quote by Leo Rosten, "...the purpose of life is to matter...to have it make some difference that we lived at all." This is her first publication.

Fostine Bright Talltree, a Native American, is presently enrolled at Peninsula College in Port Angeles, Washington. She had been a Student Council Representative for the sophomores, minorities, and re-entry students. Her work has appeared in college publications and she has also read several times at the college. Through her poetry, she makes use of her fantasies, memories, and tribal lore to weave common threads which unite her with other women. Her poetry is "eerie, haunting, and deliciously full of seductiveness." Fostine was born and raised in Port Townsend and has a 12 year old son, Michael.

Loretta Tollefson's roots are buried deep in the soil of the Olympic Mountains, where her parents live in the log home which her grandfather built and which she was raised in. A published short story writer and poet, she has just finished her first novel which is set in the puget Sound region. She lives in Seattle with her husband, who is also a writer.

Helma Swan Ward, the daughter of Makah Chief Charles Swan, was carefully trained by her father in all manner of traditional lore about her family and her tribe. She was active as a potlatch dancer in her younger years and has recently become a respected singer. Because of her strong interest in preserving the knowledge of her people, Mrs. Ward began a collaboration with anthropologist and ethnomusicologist Linda J. Goodman. A mutual friend, Libby Peck, a teacher in Queets, Washington, introduced Professor Goodman and Mrs. Ward in the summer of 1974. The two gradually struck up a friendship and decided to collaborate on the story of Mrs. Ward's life and music.
Mrs. Ward presently works in the Makah Language Program at Neah Bay, Washington and teaches Makah culture classes in the Neah Bay Public Schools.

Connie Wieneke has lived in Port Townsend for the last seven years, though is recently residing in Jackson, Wyoming where she is a reporter-special section editor for the **Jackson Hole News**. She is interested in doing free-lance writing/photography work on women in sports.

Karen Wilks was an editorial assistant to this publication. She has had extensive experience in sexuality counseling, alcohol treatment and crises-line work. She is a mother and of Native American and Black heritage.

Julie Zander is a Port Angeles resident, formerly of Connecticut, Arizona, New York, California, and Tacoma, who has written since her early teens. She studied English in Connecticut and was editor of **Dimension**, a magazine of art and writing. She works now as a counselor in a Day Treatment Center in Port Angeles.

BOOKS FROM EMPTY BOWL

Empty Bowl books are distributed by Bookslinger of Minneapolis.

EMPTY BOWL is a nonprofit organization and writers' cooperative.